America at War

World War I Through the Tabloids

Edited by
Vincent W. Rospond

[illegible]
Cover by [illegible]
This edition published [illegible]

Winged Hussar [illegible]

Winged Hussar Publishing [illegible]
[illegible]
Point Pleasant, NJ [illegible]

ISBN 978-0-98969[illegible]
LCN 2014058940

Bibliographical [illegible]
1. History [illegible]

Winged Hussar Publishing [illegible]
for more information
Visit us at [illegible]

Twitter: [illegible]
Facebook: Winged [illegible]

America At War: World War I through the Tabloids by Vincent W. Rospond
Cover by Jan Kostka
This edition published in 2021

Winged Hussar is an imprint of

Winged Hussar Publishing, LLC
1525 Hulse Rd, Unit 1
Point Pleasant, NJ 08742

Copyright © Vincent W. Rospond
ISBN 978-0-989692-66-3
LCN 2014958940

Bibliographical References and Index
1. History. 2. America. 3. World War I

Winged Hussar Publishing, LLC All rights reserved
For more information
Visit us at www.wingedhussarpublishing.com

Twitter: WingHusPubLLC
Facebook: Winged Hussar Publishing LLC

This book is sold subject to the condition that it shall not, by way of trade or otherwise, be lent, resold, hired out, or otherwise circulated without the publisher's prior consent in any form of binding or cover other than that in which it is published and without a similar condition, including this condition, being imposed on the subsequent purchaser.

The scanning, uploading, and distribution of this book via the Internet or via any other means without the permission of the publisher is illegal and punishable by law. Please purchase only authorized electronic editions, and do not participate in or encourage electronic piracy of copyrighted materials. Your support of the author's and publisher's rights is appreciated. Karma, its everywhere.

Contents

Introduction	2
Chronology of the War	4
The US in 1918	7
The Allies	25
The Auxiliaries	54
The Enemies	60
Doughboys	66
On the Eastern Front	88
Propaganda	94
The Wounded	114
Incidents of War	124
Gas Attacks	132
Artillery	138
Weapons and Equipment	148
Vehicles and Infernal Machines	159
The Air War	166
On the Water	188
People of Note	208
Places	220
Select Bibliography	

INTRODUCTION

American at War comes from a series of scrap books my great Uncle Felix Rospond collected while my grandfather served in World War One from 1917 till 1918. Uncle Felix was a meticulous person who put tried to cover the areas of American involvement during the war, and especially as it affected his older brother.

Going through the pages, which are currently crumbling through age, the story of the war, seen through American eyes is reflected in the photos affixed in place. But, this is not only a story of war it is also a story of how America viewed the war and conducted their lives. The period this scrapbook covers, dates from April through September 1918. You won't see even-handed journalism, in fact the pictures will make a point of showing how the central powers were cruel and the allied countries were noble, but the central theme is definitely about "our boys".

From a historical perspective please consider that much of what was shown was a wonder of the day. During the American Civil War, the Spanish American War, or even the Boer War, the coverage was primarily through illustrations. Placing a discernable photograph into a magazine or newspaper on a wide-scale basis was introduced in the 1890's but it is primarily a 20th century phenomenon. Many of these photos were printed using the Rotogravure process which only became popular in Newspapers and magazines like, *The Illustrated London News*, in 1912. Prior to this illustrators used photographs such as Roger Fenton's during the Crimean War or Mathew Brady's during the American Civil War and made illustrations out of them for printing. There were photographs taken of war from the Crimean War onward, but these were only shown in exhibitions.

Consider that this was an era of new, wondrous and terrible inventions. Airplanes, tractors and tanks were things out of HG Wells science fiction at a time when more than forty-percent of Americans lived in rural areas and travelling by horse and carriage was still considered fairly common. This showcase journalism acted as a way to promote the might of the allied war effort and the US industry There are gas-masks that look medieval armor and aerial views of towns that people had never seen before the airplane which became a wonderment to the reading public.

This was also a private war played out in public. In previous wars, the names of casualties might have appeared in newspapers or at the news office on what were known as "casualty roles". In this conflict the pictures of those who had given their lives took up whole pages of the papers and magazines to tell the tale of the diversity of people supporting the war. The irony of this is that a portion of these people did not share rights equally – women did not even have the right to vote until 1920. African-Americans were present in the field, but not very visible in the news. Service men in the field "mugged" for the camera in whimsical ways and showed off for the folks back home.

This was also a heavily censored war. The US government let information get through that it wanted. Letters home were often censored – not only for locations the men were in, but how they were feeling. It is also important to remember that many photos were filtered through government agencies which showed what they wanted when they wanted.

Most importantly, consider this is the cross-roads of an era for America, when it sprang from a second-rate to world power. It was a time when American Civil War Veterans still paraded down Broadway in the Memorial Day parades, where sheep grazed on the White House

Lawn and people were encouraged to plant gardens. At the same time there are great steel shipyards, mighty munitions factories and food to feed the hungry of the world. From a twenty-first century perspective this may all seem "cute" and "quaint", but at the time many of these photos were of state of the art items and facilities.

The material I was working from to put this together, range from glossy magazines to rag-paper newsprint. Where possible I have tried to credit the photographers or agencies where possible, but some photos simply didn't have credits to cite. Each photo will include the caption as well as an entry to place the photo in context or provide additional information. It is an example of an American view of the war and how it was presented.

My grandfather's family came through Ellis Island in the first decade of the twentieth century, but my uncle was the only one born here. When they arrived here from Galicia, they became 100% American, there was no going back. When war was declared, my grandfather joined up even though at his age he was probably low in the list to be drafted. He served the war in France and when he returned from the war he never held a grudge against the common soldiers who he fought against, but there were always reminders from the war haunted him (th smell of cooked cheese reminded him of trenchfoot). When World War II broke out he tried to join up again, but was too old, so he was a welder in the Bayonne shipyards, but he always tried to help veterans.

Before ending I want to thanks Dr. Adrian Mandzy PhD for his help on some of the background material, especially on the Hetmanate, and his review of my early ramblings.

This is a snapshot of the war and how it was viewed. I hope you enjoy it.

Vincent W. Rospond

CHRONOLOGY OF WAR (Highlights)

1914
28 June – The heir to the Austrian throne Archduke Franz Ferdinand is assassinated in Sarajevo
1 August – Germany declares war on Russia
3 August – Germany declares war on France and demands free passage through Belgium
4 August – Belgium is invaded and Britain declares war on Germany
16 August – Germans capture Liége
19 October – 17 November – First Battle of Ypres

1915
22 April – 25 May – Second Battle of Ypres
***7 May* - the SS. *Lusitania* is sunk by a German U-Boat**
29 September – French capture the crest of Vimy Ridge

1916
21 February – 18 December – the Battle of Verdun
14 March - 7 February 1917 - Expedition against Pancho Villa
1 July – 18 November – Battle of the Somme
30 July - the Black Tom explosion, Jersey City, NJ (likely German saboteurs)

1917
January - Germany unleashes unrestricted submarine warfare / Zimmerman Telegram
9 March - US recognizes the Provisional Russian Government
6 April - US declares War on the German Empire
9 – 14 April – Battle of Vimy
16-20 April – Nivelle Offensive
June - First American troops arrive in France
7-14 June – Battle of Messines
1 July – The Kerensky Offensive
19 July – German counter-attack in Russia
31 July – 10 November – Third Battle of Ypres
3 September – German Capture of Riga
12 October – First Battle of Passchendaele
26 October – 10 November – Second Battle of Passchendaele
20 November – 7 December – Battle of Cambrai
7 December - US declares war on Austria-Hungary, but never declares on the other Central Powers

1918
15 January - US I Corps is made Operational
21 February – British capture Jericho
24 February - US II Corps is made Operational
21 March – 5 April – 'Michael Offensive'/Second Battle of the Somme

21 – 3 March – Battle of St Quentin
28 May – Battle of Cantigny
2 – 4 June – Battle of Château –Thierry
11 – 12 June – Battle of Belleau Wood
15-23 June – Battle of Piave
2 July – Italian advance on Piave
8 – 11 August – Battle of Amiens
12 – 16 September – Battle of St Mihiel
19 September – Battle of Megiddo or Samaria
26 September – 11 November – Meuse Argonne Offensive
28 September – 11 November – Flanders Offensive
17 October – 11 November – Picardy Offensive
11 November - Armistice

Bolded items are specific to the US

World War I through the Tabloids

The US in 1918

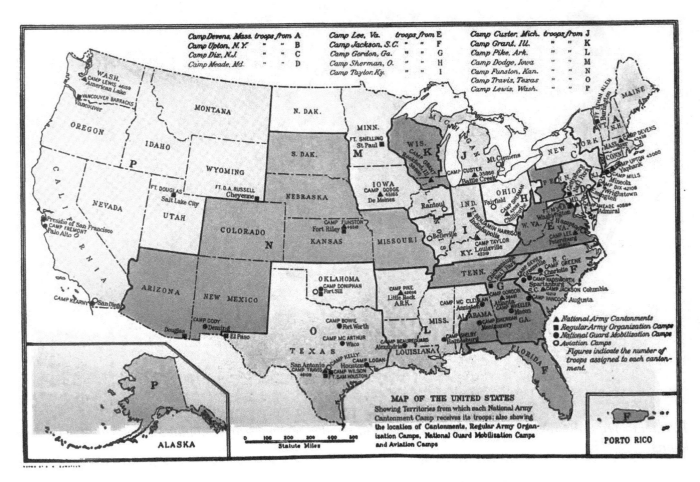

Army Camps in the US during World War I

America at War

The United States that entered World War I was not prepared to field a modern army. Except for U-boats in the Atlantic, Black Tom and the fear of spies, the war did not really touch the American mainland. None-the-less, the nation threw itself wholly behind the war effort. Patriotic men volunteered, families economized, and the nation glowed in its history of freedom and war. Differing from World War II and subsequent conflicts, President Wilson was not front and center for every occasion. This was a time when presidents were low key and stayed in the background. The main cheerleader for the government at war was the Secretary of War – Newton Baker.

1. *The Liberty Ball crossing 23rd Street on the last lap of the journey from Buffalo to New York for Liberty Loans.*

(previous page) "Liberty Bonds" and private donations helped to finance the war effort as in previous conflicts. The cost of war was, however, much more expensive. In the American Civil War, bonds were a major source of funding allowing the government to fight the war. The three years prior to the United States entering the war, the country had made a significant amount of money selling arms and material to the combatants, as well as providing financing. But, it would be the private citizens of the US that helped provide funding for the armed forces. Gimmicks like the "Liberty Ball", a wire ball used to collect money from citizens for the war effort coincided with "Bond Drives" where celebrities would exhort crowds of people to give money. This was still an era of "personal" appeals.

2. *Shropshire Sheep on the White House lawn.*

Sheep were kept on the lawn to maintain its appearance as well provide meat for the White House table. It was meant to show even the President was doing what he could to economize as the nation went into a war economy. Citizens were encouraged to plant vegetable gardens, though it was not the same as the rationing experienced in World War II. There were still drives for meatless days, collecting metal and even peach pits which were used in gas masks.

3. Secretary Baker presenting the diploma of graduation to Cadet John Paul Dean of Worchester, Mass, the Honor Man of the Class of 1919. (Times Photo Service)

Dean was appointed to the Army Corps of Engineers as a Brevet Captain in June 1918. He served at Camp Humphrey's in VA and then an instructor at West Point.

Secretary Baker was always in the forefront of the War effort – often in uniform even though he had no official rank. Baker never served in the military and was chided before April 1917 as being a pacifist. He was a strong supporter of the League of Nations after the war and was considered a potential presidential candidate in the 1920's and 30's. He was used by President's Coolidge and Hoover to represent the US in Europe.

4. Newarkers, aroused by the U-boats dirty work, rush to enlist in the navy. They are shown taking the oath at the Park Place recruiting station. The station is at 86 Park Place near the McAdoo Terminal.

The Newark Evening News (1883 – 1972) focused on the happenings of the city that rivaled New York City in the early part of the century. At this time, Newark, NJ was a vibrant community as a hub for shipping, train and trucking. McAdoo terminal referred to is most likely the present-day Penn Station. The present location is empty, part of the greenspace.

America at War

5. Men chosen in the selective service from Harlem march down Broadway toward the National Army Camp. (International Film)

Even though there was a draft, many men signed up for service as a sign a patriotism. The papers and films reinforced this idea to encourage enlistment. The draft originally focused on men 21 to 30 and later expanded to men 18 to 45. More than two million men volunteered and five million were drafted. Although three years of war had dampened the enthusiasm of Europeans, Americans greeted men who had signed up as if it was 1914.

6. *Racing season opened at the Jamaica Racetrack in Queens, NY. On May 16th. The featured race was the Paumonok Handicap won by Old Koenig, Startling second and the favorite Campfire third. (Western Newspaper Union).*

Once the US entered the war there was some discussion of whether sports would continue as before the war. Although many athletes enlisted in the military, it was not on the scale of World War II. Life still continued as before. Five professional baseball players were killed in action and several more were injured including star pitcher Christy Mathewson who injured his lungs in a mock gas attack. The Paumonok Handicap was run annually with some exceptions from 1906 to 1959 at the Jamaica Racetrack. The race is currently held at Aqueduct Racetrack.

7. *Grace Carley (Mrs. Oliver Harriman) was a leading socialite fishing as part of the self-reliant movement.*

Grace Carley's husband was a leading New York financier who was part of the New York National Guard in his youth. She identified as Chairman of the Mayor John Haylan's "Mayor's Committee for Women on National Defense" which served as an early version of the USO. Millicent Hearst was also list as Chairman of this committee at different points. At a time when society women did not engage in "sports" fishing was considered a way to feed the family.

8. The oldest man in the Navy and his grandson. Adolph L. Lowe, 77, served from 1861 to 1865, and reenlisted as a Carpenter's Mate on May 29, 1917. The grandson, Gaston V. Lowe is serving on a battleship. (Committee on Public Information)

Another example of generations doing their part to defend the country. The call for volunteers pulled at the strings of patriotism across generations. It was a time when men were asked to join what was often termed a righteous crusade to make the world safe for democracy. In 1940, Gaston V. Lowe was still living in Paterson, NJ

World War I through the Tabloids

9. Part of the ever-thinning blue line in the Memorial Day parade. Added solemnity was given to the occasion by the fact that our men are fighting and casualty lists grow daily. (International Film)

This was originally called Decoration Day, starting in the 1880's it was sometimes called, "Memorial Day", though this was not officially changed until an act of Congress in 1967. The wounds of the American Civil War had not quite fully healed, and the government hoped that military action similar to the appeal of the Spanish-American war would help bring people back together. Woodrow Wilson was a small boy from Virginia during the war, who met Robert E. Lee at his father's farm.

10. Thrilling incident of the Memorial Day parade on Riverside; the six sole surviving Zouaves, daredevil civil war fighters carrying their tattered flags. (International Film)

The 5th New York Zouaves also known as Duryée's Zouaves served from 1861 to 1863. Veteran's later re-enrolled in the 5th New York Veteran Volunteer Infantry. Memorial Day in 1918 still contained Civil War Veterans. Veterans would march and have reunions with Blue and Gray joining hands. They would still have large reunions into the 1930's. The last veteran died in 1959

11. This section of the paper was called, "The Field of Honor". The soldiers who gave their lives were shown, what unit they were in and how they died. More than 4 million men joined the war for the US, while 65,000 died - some in action, some in accidents and some from disease. Soldiers still died from diseases, and to complicate things the Influenza of 1918 also hit the soldiers in Europe and the US.

America at War

Private Alfred Ferguson, 308th Inf., New York. Died in France.

Private John Peters, an Indian, Engineers Corps, Keshena, Wis. Killed in action.

Lieut. Aimee D. Genard, 103rd Inf., Manchester, N. H. Killed in accident in France.

Lieut. Albert E. Johnson, 102nd Inf., Collinsville, Conn. Killed in action.

As you can see soldiers came from all walks of life, and all ranks. These soldiers are mostly from the Northeast.

World War I through the Tabloids

Lester Sweete, who has taken up intensive farming in anticipation of the anti-loafing law. Armed with an automobile horn he is hard at work, scaring the crows from his cornfield.

12. Comics had been used in American politics and war since the American Revolution. By the late nineteenth century comics made a regular appearance in newspapers and magazines for entertainment. During the war they were used to give irony to situations Americans found themselves in. It was a way to find comfort and humor.

13. The optimist - "Gee whiz, Mrs. Brown! You ought not to feel sad about your son being in France. Just look at me - why, I haven't seen my 'Gran' in California for four months."

World War I through the Tabloids

14. Another example of humor in the realities of war.

"I don't want to get drafted on a farm with all them hicks; I'd rather go over'n join Pershing." The bunch around the Palace Hotel bar talking over the chances of being put on a war job.

15. Abie the Agent was a Yiddish character created by Harry Hershfeld concerning Yiddishism and Jewish immigrants in the United States starting in 1914. The main character was Abraham Kabibble, known as Abie the Agent, was the first Jewish protagonist of an American comic strip. Abie's humorous caricature was a rebuttal of some of the Jewish stereotypes in caricatures and represented a moderately successful middle-class immigrant. Abie and his friends lacked many of the negative or malicious elements, such as exaggerated physical traits, found in the depictions of Jews from this time. Abie was in many ways indistinguishable from other Americans, and he was a prime example of the belief in the integration of German Jews into U.S. society. During 1917, the character enlisted in the United States Army to help the U.S. forces in World War I.

World War I through the Tabloids 23

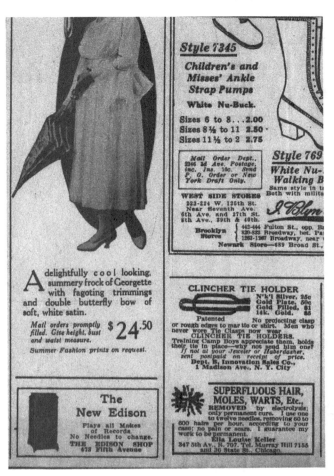

16. A sample of advertisements as life went on in the midst of war. Clincher tie holders and hair removal were popular items.

The Allies

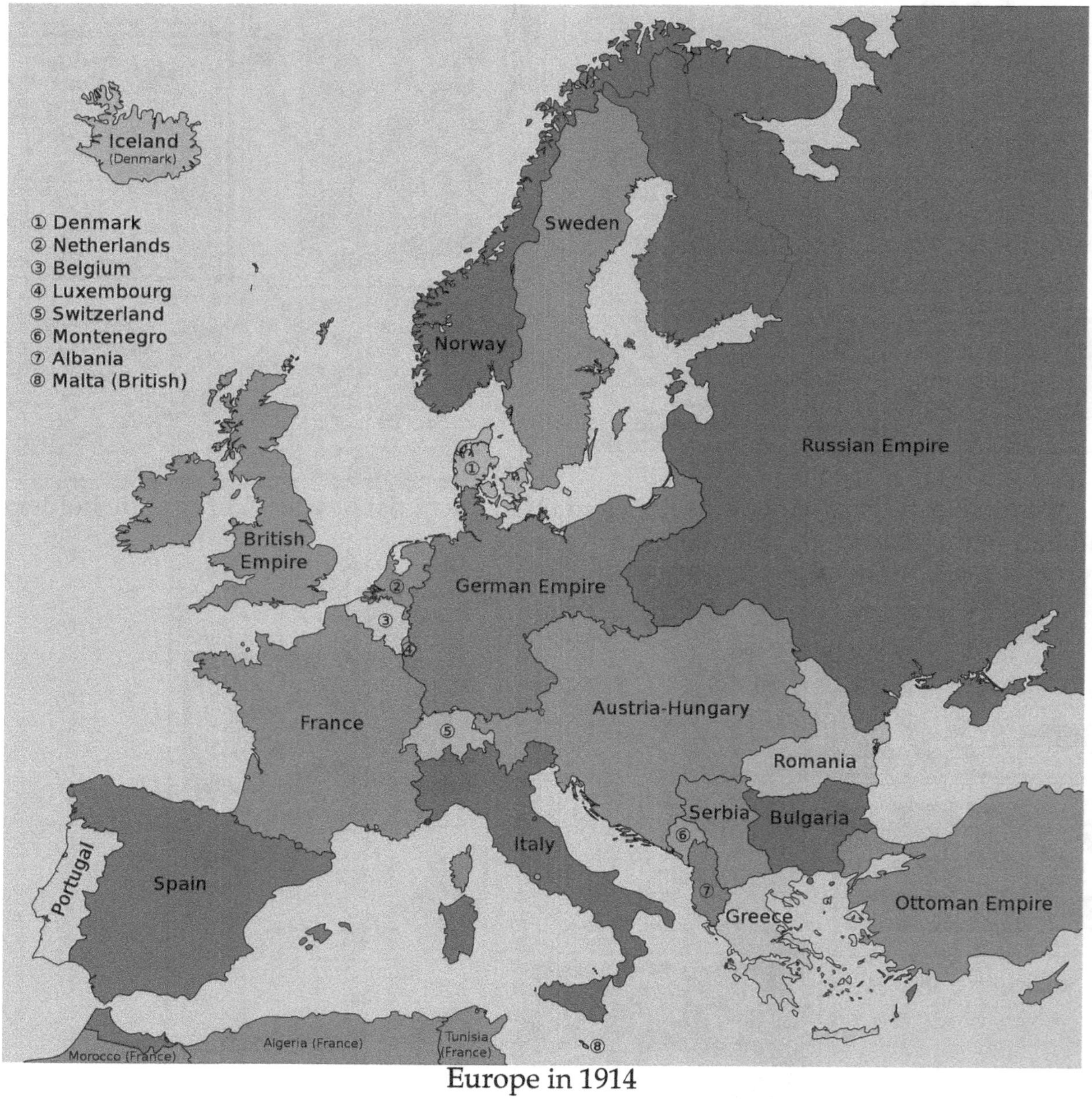
Iceland
(Denmark)
① Denmark
② Netherlands
③ Belgium
④ Luxembourg
⑤ Switzerland
⑥ Montenegro
⑦ Albania
⑧ Malta (British)
Sweden
Norway
Russian Empire
British Empire
German Empire
Austria-Hungary
France
Romania
Serbia
Bulgaria
Italy
Portugal
Spain
Greece
Ottoman Empire
Algeria (France)
Tunisia (France)
Morocco (France)

Europe in 1914

World War I through the Tabloids

The Allies were – well the Allies. They were the nations the United States joined to protect democracy. They were a large group of nations (and some soon to be nations) that spanned the world. The news media showed victorious allies fighting on multiple front with all the might of a modern war that incorporated elements of traditional conflicts. The allies were honorable and gentlemanly as opposed to the dastardly and cruel Central Powers. Most importantly, the Allies were all into the war and the defeat of the enemy.

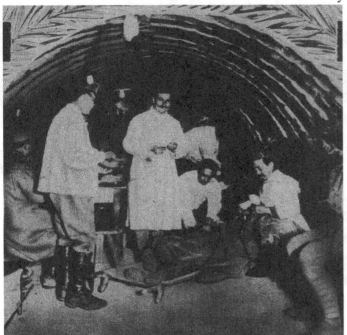

17. Even the hospitals are not spare by the vandal Teutons and quarters bearing the Red Cross emblem must be as well as protected as the trenches and dugouts themselves. This surgical hospital near the fighting line in the Aisne district is many feet underground, and even then the desperately wounded are not safe from Hun bombardment (Committee on Public Information)

The overriding theme that was propagates by the allies from the start of the war was the cruelty of the Central Powers towards civilians and soldiers.

18. (below) The Polish-American volunteers is shown here marching to the front in France. It contains many Newarkers. Every man and officer is a volunteer. (Underwood and Underwood)

One of President Wilson's Fourteen Points speech in January 1918 was the restoration of Poland. Earlier than this, volunteers in the Austrian, Prussian and Russian armies had raised "Polish" units for their own propaganda use. The unit pictured here was part of Gen. Haller's "Blue Army" raised in France wearing the French horizon blue uniforms, but with Polish four-cornered caps. This group has a flag with a Polish eagle. There was a large group of Polish immigrants on the east coast of the US – some joined this unit, many joined up as US doughboys.

19/20. Women soldiers who were in the trenches on the Russian Front. Below, four survivors of the Battalion of Death out of a company of two hundred. (Red Cross Mission to Russia). This picture does not identify which unit it is, but most likely it is the 1st Russian Woman's battalion of Death which was engaged in the Kerensky Offensive in May 1917.

Even though the article this picture comes from was published in 1918, the contributions of Russia were still played up. There were fifteen formations named "Battalion of Death" composed of all women that were formed in 1917 to make up for manpower in war weary Russia. In the time of socialist/pre-communist Russia, there was more openness towards equality of the sexes. The 1st battalion actually did very well in combat but were not supported when they went into action. It would appear that the 1st Russian Woman's Battalion did not exceed three hundred soldiers in total when they went into combat. The four women pictured were actually not the only survivors, but among the survivors. By 1918 some of these units became auxiliary units, others fought on both sides of the revolution. In the top picture you can see several male officers among the battalion personnel.

21. *On guard in the marshes. It makes a pretty picture, but the Belgian sentinel who is guarding the road to the outpost probably found the situation rather lonely and uncomfortable. (Central News)*

The water table in Flanders (French speaking Belgium) was high, meaning you could not dig very deep before hitting water. This Belgian soldier has a cover over his French Adrian steel helmet.

22. *Formerly used to summon the people of a little French town to church, this bell is now serving as a warning signal to the inhabitants against German poison gas attacks. (Official French Photo)*

More than likely the church that the bell served was no longer whole. The threat of poison gas was real in that it could not be controlled. Gas was delivered by artillery shells or by releasing it into the air and letting the wind carry it. The problem is when the wind changed direction, the gas could go back towards the attackers. Another problem with gas it that it always sought the lowest level so that while it may have appeared to have passed, it often lingered in depressions, shell holes and trenches.

23. (previous page) *Both French and British cavalry played a prominent part in stopping the first German rush in the great German offensive in the west. Here British cavalry reserves, ready to act as infantry, waiting for the call – I.F.S*

Early in the war, British cavalry were ready for the breakthrough that never came. By late 1915 some had traded in their horses for the trenches. Even in 1914, cavalry had become more mounted infantry than knights of the battlefield. Often, they would ride to a location and take positions as infantry. There were still several cavalry battles – in the early war at Mons and the Marne. On the eastern front and in Arabia cavalry still fought a combination of traditional charges and mounted infantry.

24. *British batteries in action in Palestine (Central News Photo Service)*

Although this is identified as a British unit, the guns look like French canon de 77 mle 1897's. The Middle East was considered a backwater area after the Gallipoli campaign, but in Arabia it was more a battle of maneuver than the western front. By 1917, there was actually more success for the Allies in Arabia than the trenches of France.

25. (next page, top) *Through and Over Water. Here is shown English soldiers in Palestine who are finding the trip vastly different from what they had seen before. The ancient country is being remodeled to suit the needs of the army and the picture shows a wooden trestle built by an Anzac regiment. Camels are used for transporting supplies. Big trains of the animals are always on the road. (By International)*

Despite mechanization movement through hostile country by animals were still the most reliable mode of transport. More than a million horses were used in a variety of capacities. This was an era where mechanization met animal.

26. (below) *Drawing of camels in the desert with the British army*

This is a continuation of the old tradition of illustrating the war that goes back to the Crimean War. Though wood cuts based on photos were used from the Crimean War in the 1850's photos didn't start being published in magazines until the 1890's. Although photos were now the main source of illustration for newspapers and magazines, they were still bulky and required relatively sedimentary subjects. Illustrators, therefore still had a value to readers to show events of the day. The British used thousands of camels to move supplies and troops during the course of the war.

27. *British Tommies going forward, bound for the trenches where the world's greatest battle is raging. (The Committee on Public Information)*

This picture later appear in another publication with the caption, "A detachment of British troop on their way to the Somme front. One would think that they were on their way to a barbecue or some other picnic frolic – but their faces will assume an entirely different expression when they get sight of the Huns.

Second Battle of the Somme, 21 August to 2 September 1918. All the guns have a protective canvas covers to protect them from the mud, including a Lewis gun in the center soldier. The second battle of the Somme was part of several engagements that included battles at Bapaume, Arras, Mount St. Quentin and Peronne. The success of the allies in this campaign played a role in the final defeat of Germany in November.

28. *Part of a trench on the Italian front held by British troops who, like the French, are helping the Italians to stop the drive by the Germans and Austrians last autumn. (Underwood & Underwood, NY)*

You can see a Lewis gun in the center and a British officer on the left in a different kit from the rest of the soldiers. This trench system is in the midst of a heavily wooded area, very unlike the bare western front. By 1918 the Italian front was supported by troops from the US, Great Britain and France, but this was not generally publicized in the western press which portrayed the allied effort as victorious up and down the line.

29. (Next page top) *British troops assembling in the city square in the war scourged city of Arras, which place the Germans have been endeavoring for nearly four years to capture. It has suffered tremendously from gun fire (International Film Service)*

Arras was six miles from the front and was in the midst of several battles, including the battle of Vimy and the second battle of the Somme. Arras is the site of two Canadian cemeteries to their World War I dead.

30. (Below) *Identified as British cavalry in Flanders.*

The figures in the front of the picture are part of the horse artillery. Those animals are most likely mules. Some breeds of horses were almost wiped out as a result of the war. Clydesdales and mules were the main workhorses of the allied effort.

30. *More British camels in Egypt*

The British army in what was then called Palestine. Water is carried through a canvas aqueduct in the foreground to troops in the field.

31. *Camel train carrying water for the British army in Palestine. The desert transport service depends in part on means used centuries ago. From a drawing by James McBey, official artist (Underwood and Underwood, NY)*

Even though this was a modern war this was still fought like wars of the 19th century – relying on vast amounts of animals. The Middle East was an exotic, far away place that was still inhabited by Bedouin raiders, Arabian Nights and Lawrence of Arabia.

32. *Canadian troops attack under smoke in Flanders.*

This is the battle of Amiens 8 – 12 August 1918. This was also known as the third battle of Picardy. Amiens kicked off what would be known as the "Hundred Days Offensive." Note, the officer in the foreground with his soft cap instead of a helmet. While many officers used a helmet in action, some – through bravado – wore the peaked soft cap in the field. This is a cropped shot of number 30 which was reused from the Battle of Courcelette

33. *Canadian troops going over the top in Flanders.*

Courageous troops are always going over the top. One of the hallmarks of the Great War was the image of brave troops "going over the top" which meant leaving the security of the trenches to charge across "no man's land" toward the enemy. After the opening campaigns of the war, such tactics were used more judiciously on the western front, but remained in the mythos of the war.

34. *Over the top at Courcelette – Canadians leaving their trenches in a dashing counterattack.*

Courcelette was a major tactical objective in the Battle of Flers-Courcelette (15-22 September 1916) during the Somme Offensive of the First World War during which the village was razed. The village was assigned as the major objective of the Canadian Corps during that battle and they succeeded in capturing it. Accordingly, the actions and sacrifices of the Canadians are commemorated at the Courcelette Memorial which is just south of the village.

35. *British cavalry in France amidst artillery and refugees.*

Even though the caption says cavalry, the horses are actually trace horses for the artillery. These were the horses used to pull the guns and wagons toward the front lines.

36. *A cave cut into the side of a cliff by French soldiers on the Oise sector – Photo by Paul Thompson.*

This was another version of the dugouts used in trenches to protect troops in the field. This was most likely used by officers. The use of caves as dugouts was as old as warfare and used depending on the ground water. Where the water table was close to the surface, trenches and defensive hideouts could not be dug deep. If the surrounding countryside allowed shelters to be dug parallel rather than down, men took advantage.

37. *Where 12,000 French war-workers eat in the famous Citroen works. Note that each has his bottle of wine (International)*

At this time in many factories the company sponsored meals for the workers – many of whom are women as the men were off to war. Women would not attain suffrage in France until 1944, but as in the case of women in other countries they started taking on jobs traditionally occupied by men.

38. *British cavalrymen dismounting to aid hard-pressed infantry during the Picardy Battle – I.F.S.*

The Battle of Amiens also known as the Third Picardy 8 August 1918. As previously discussed, cavalry often fought as infantry in the trenches.

39. *The camp of Chabrias in Egypt, begun by Romans two thousand years ago and finished by the Australians yesterday. A mouth of the Nile once gave it importance (Underwood & Underwood)*

The war did not directly make it to the inland of Egypt, but it was always on the border of war against the Ottomans. British Commonwealth troops set up camps in the interior.

40. *A fight in a French town*

This drawing has an odd mixture of blue uniforms with steel helmets. More heroic than accurate. It was important for the western powers in general and the US in particular after they entered the war, to show the heroism of troops in battle – real and imagined. The Germans pictured to the left are pictured wearing uniforms from the Franco-Prussian War.

41. *A British Tommy drinks to the health of his Poilu friend. While they may not be able to understand each other's language, there is not the slightest doubt about their understanding each other's sentiments (International Film Service)*

By this time in the war, the British and French had been fighting more than four year and in some of the most brutal fighting to date. It was important for the allied press to show the camaraderie of the major powers.

42. *Nothing is more sacred to a soldier than his regimental colors. Some of the really wonderful deed of daring have been performed to save the flag from the foe. Here a French Colonel is himself carrying the shell torn standard from the Picardy battle.*

Despite the image the paper is trying to portray of troops carrying their colors into battle, they were more likely to be kept at the regimental HQ in the field, away from the action. Some units did carry flags into action in the opening months of the war, but casualties and damage from fire made the colors too exposed.

World War I through the Tabloids

43. *French Poilu charges in Flanders*

What may or may not be a posed photo of a Poilu in light equipment. By this stage in the war troops attacked in light equipment. Early in the war when generals kept anticipating a breakthough they might have full packs, but that was quickly lost when going "over the top" or on patrol.

44. *Photo taken somewhere in the Somme sector showing a detail of French soldiers lying in ambush for a German patrol that is reconnoitering for information concerning French trenches and to what extent they are defended (Kadel & Herbert)*

Troops in action were in demand by the Homefront in the newsreels and on the papers. Once an area was the center of battle all cover was lost, forcing troops to find cover in depressions in the land. Patrols were a constant process – usually at night – to keep the enemy from finding out about the trenches in front of them. It was important for attacking troops to know the terrain they were attacking. Defending troops often transformed the landscape behind their forward trenches. Raids were a common occurrence to gain knowledge and prisoners.

45. *A supporting wave of French shock troops during an advance on a formidable German blockhouse. The barrage fire having lifted, the men are making their way forward to the assault. (Kadel & Herbert)*

Rolling or creeping barrages wee used to attack enemy lines. The artillery would slowly make its way toward the enemy line with the infantry advancing behind it. Once it passed the attack point, it would proceed beyond to discourage a counter-attack by infantry. In theory this was how it worked, but without proper maps and communication, especially early in the war, this was not as effective as planned. Once a proper development of air strategy combined arms made this type of attack more effective.

46. (top next page) *This photograph was taken at a critical period of the great German drive into Italy and shows a body of French troops passing through an Italian city to relieve the hard-pressed forces of General Diaz on the Piave (Photo Press Illustrating Service)*

The second battle of the Piave River was fought from 15-23 June 1918. It was the first major offensive of Austro-Hungarian forces after the withdrawal of Russia from the war, which allowed them to move more forces to the southern front. It resulted in a defeat for the Austro-Hungarian forces. The Italians were supported by three British and two French Divisions. The Germans had hoped increased pressure would force the allies to use American troops from the western front to counter the attack, but this was not necessary.

47. (Below) *On the way back to the fighting line – French soldiers who have been resting near Choisy-la-Victoire after doing their part in the battle of Flanders returning to the front again to take part in the struggle. (Choisy-la-Victoire is a town in north-east France)*

Even though there are trucks on the road, the infantry is marching to the front. Several of the French soldiers – with full packs – have walking sticks. They wore their packs until they got into the line then kept them in their dugouts and bivouacs.

48. *There may be a shortage of man power in France, but the nation manages to keep formidable its activities on many fronts. Here is a scene in Morocco with a big gun operated by Colonials in action at Touahar against rebellious tribesmen.*

World War I ignited a new wave of nationalism in Europe and the Middle East, but Morocco was and would continue to be a hotbed of anti-French feeling amongst the tribesmen. Touahar is Touahria in Mostaganem Province in Algeria. After the war, this was the area that made the French Foreign Legion famous.

49. Indian troops passing through the streets of Baghdad on their way to join the British forces on the fighting front. The loyalty of the Indians has been a great help to the Allies in numerous circumstances.

Iraq was part of the Ottoman Empire known as Mesopotamia, which was invaded by British troops from Persia (Iran). After some initial setbacks, the British sent more than 120,000 troops there to control the region and after the war the British created the Kingdom of Iraq out but controlled the administration of the country.

50. *In the long period of inactivity since the last Teuton offensive, the Italian army has been put in fine condition. The photograph shows Italian marines, specially trained as shock troops, carrying an important Austrian position.*

This might actually be troops in action, taken a safe distance away. The area of operation is most likely the Piave River campaign, the battle of Vitoria Veneto. This was fought from 24 October to 3 November 1918 and resulted in an Italian victory.

51. *Fortifications in Italy built above ground instead of dug below, and the troops live in the fortified sections.*

It looks as if the army made us of an existing city wall to build up a defensive line around it. Due to the rock nature of the terrain in northern Italy digging down was not always possible. This necessitated some cases of building up defensive works

52. *How Italians transport food over Mountains. Overcoming the difficulties of transit which complicates mountain warfare, the Italians are here shown transporting wine and food to the front lines by aerial ferry. Each carriage permits the transportation of considerable supplies.* (in the original text the "f" was left off of the words "of")

A great deal of the fighting on the Italian Front was in mountainous areas. This required moving supplies in the same manner as cable cars through a series of lifts. The fighting shown on this photo most likely corresponds to the Piave River campaign.

53. *On the Canadian front in France. German shells are exploding just beyond a pile of the debris of war (British Official Photo)*

That debris includes pieces of tanks and vehicles.

54. *German intrigue attempted to foment a rebellion in India, but loyal troops squelched the uprising. A scouting party of Nepalese infantry is shown here at work (International Film)*

Both sides in the war tried to exploit nationalist aspirations within the enemy camps. On the whole the allies seem to have done a better job, but the comradery of war brought aspirations of independence to the forefront. Soon after the war many of the Commonwealth troops began lobbying for their own voice.

55. *Still in the Ring. Still battling bravely against the army that has wrought such ruin in their country, Serbian soldiers are shown here manning an anti-aircraft gun. It will be noticed that the gun is but a field piece improvised to combat air raiders, which proves the indomitable Serbian spirit.*

The war essentially started over Serbia, and they were quickly overrun, but their small army continued to fight with the allies. They saw action in Bulgaria and Macedonia, fighting alongside Greek and British troops.

56. *Yes, they have telephones and every other modern convenience in Japan just the same as here. The scene is laid in the Tokio (sic) Exchange (Press Illustrating Service)*

This is interesting from the point that the news needed to show how the ally Japan was a modern country, and underneath that – all the operators are wearing kimonos – a mix of old and new.

57. *An Italian official photograph showing a lot of wounded men receiving medical attention at a first aid station and awaiting ambulances to carry them to the field hospital. The Italian Red Cross and medical corps is fully equipped and trained to a remarkable degree of efficiency and compare favorably with any other branch of the organization in Europe. The Italian soldier is a wonderful combination of grit and endurance, particularly these hardy mountaineers who belong in the Alps and who are fighting with steadfast determination to protect their beloved Venice against the ruthless invaders who threaten to destroy it (Western Newspaper Union)*

This was also the Piave River Campaign. The fighting on the Italian front was a series of battles that went back and forth, but usually consisted of Italy losing ground, then winning it back. By 1918 a combination of support from the allies and pressure on the Germans and Austrians allowed the Italian front to start making gains.

58. *"Are we downhearted? I should say not!" is Tommy's answer as he marches forward light-heartedly in his fight for world freedom. And now that the American troops are with them, they are happier still. (International Film Service)*

These are enthusiastic British troops on the way to the front. The press never showed anything else but determined or enthusiastic troops.

59. *THE ALLIES SECONDARY DEFENCE – Military strategists, in their calculations, should not overlook the hoodoo effect of these British mascots on the German army – British official, from Gilliams Service. Bill will stand for anything – except the acquisition of Mitteleuropa by the Central Powers.*

During wars soldiers will sometimes adopt animals as mascots that served with the unit such as "Old Abe" and eagle of the 8th Wisconsin Volunteer Infantry in the American Civil War who supposedly flew overhead during battle and returned to his perch after the fighting. During the lull of fighting and at headquarters some units kept animals as pets that became unit mascots. In most cases they were a form of gallows humor. Sometimes they were used to make fun of officers, some the war and some just the companionship under terrible circumstances. Occasionally they were raised as food.

World War I through the Tabloids

60. (Right) *Just a dog, but he may have influence.*

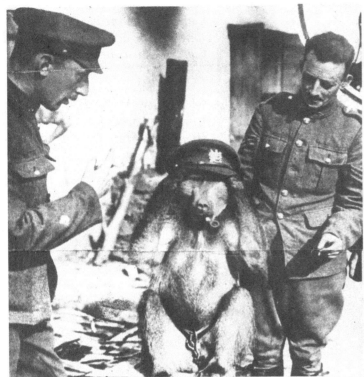

61. (Left) *This veteran (Baboon) landed in Belgium with the Royal Engineers in 1914 and was present at Ypres and Loos. He has been wounded and is now on leave in Italy.*

62. (Below) *The Royal Welsh Fusiliers are training this Angora goat*

63. (Left) *Seated on a captured German mortar is Charles Darwin, in the act of hoodooing all German guns of that type.*

64. (Below) *The Royal Flying Corps has great faith in the ability of its rabbits to show Germany her place.*

65. (Right) Scottish unit's mascot

Auxiliaries

Auxiliaries for the Army and Navy were covered by professional and civilian components. Although civilian nurses had been part of the armed forces since the colonial era, they were never officially part of the government forces. During the American Civil War there were female nurses, but they were volunteers under the direction of Dorthea Dix. Following the Spanish-American War a bill was introduced to Congress for the creation of the Army Nurse Corps (1901), followed by the Navy Nurse Corps in (1908). The Red-Cross acted as the clearing house for nurses from 1905 onward.

When the U.S. entered the war, more than 20,000 nurses were recruited for service with more than half serving overseas. The nurses were assigned to fifty-eight military hospitals and staffed forty-seven ambulance companies. During this period over five thousand women enrolled in the Army's Nursing School.

Volunteer organizations such as the Salvation Army set up positions near the front lines to provide coffee and comfort for the troops. The Red Cross also played a role in helping U.S. troops overseas. Although the many of these groups were often in harm's way, they were not eligible for decorations. An overriding theme of the papers seems to have been how cruelly the Germans acted towards nurses and civilian auxiliaries.

66. *American nurse on a train – This ambulance train, built for the American Army was on exhibition at Waterloo Station, London. The proceeds of the exhibition went to St. Dunstan's Hospital.*

Hospital trains and ships where marked with a giant red cross. That did not mean they were immune from harm. Most hits were probably unintentional, but it was exploited for propaganda purposes. The hospital trains (Ambulance Trains) became more efficient as the war progressed and the saved lives by getting wounded from the front lines to the care quickly.

67. *American nurses in France* – *A group of American nurses in front of their headquarters at Toul, the principal town of the American zone in the Lorraine region. These girls have been taking care of Pershing's men who were wounded in the recent fighting there. (Underwood & Underwood)*

Although the Army wanted to keep nurses out of harms way they did the most good close to the front line. As a consequence, nurses wee injured or killed during the course of the war.

68. *Salvation Army workers making pies at the front lines for American soldiers equipped with a "Tin" hat and gas mask (Committee on Public Information)*

The Salvation Army workers were neither "Army" no "nurses", but filled a vital function to the morale of US troops.

69. Native American Red Cross workers – the caption lists them as, *Squaws, at one time noted dancers in the old Mono Indian celebrations of the far west, who now, at nearly eighty-five years each have become Red Cross Workers for America.*

70. British Auxiliaries working in a munitions plant – *Women are more and more finding their place in warring countries. These comprise the fire fighting force at a big British munitions plant. They have proved most efficient firemen (Central News Photo Service)*

Women did not get the vote in Britain until 1918 and the U.S. in 1920, but World War I accelerated the right for women to vote. As men went to war, women filled the gap in a variety of positions and did it just as well – which did not go unnoticed.

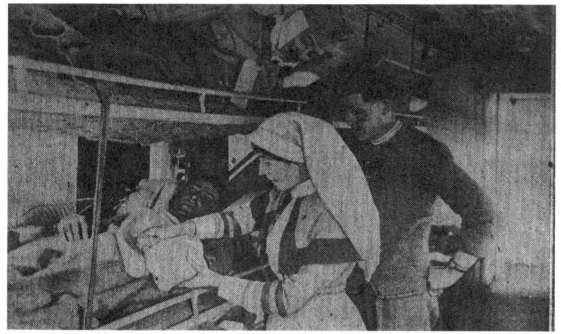

71. British Nurses assisting on an Army train – Tender Hands of Mercy – These wounded soldiers are being taken to a base hospital on board a British ambulance train somewhere in France. The stretchers are slung along the sides of the car and are non-oscillating, thus insuring the greatest comfort to the injured. (British Official Photo)

Hospital trains were specially outfitted to shuttle wounded men. These stretchers were fixed in place to keep men secure. (See the section on, "The Wounded".

72. Red Cross using a farmhouse to as a hospital – There are many picturesque scenes, but none greater than this Red Cross station in the line. The shell shattered farmhouse besides the lake has been taken over for surgeons and stretcher bearers.

This is an example of a forward dressing station. Red Cross facilities were set up in triage system where the most serious were stabilized and passed up the line to the facilities that could best service them.

73. *American women helping to rebuild a village – American women are reconstructing this village in the Department of Meurthe along the Moselle, destroyed by the Hun in 1914. Lumber, stone and tile are shown ready for the workmen.*

These women were not part of the army, but Salvation Army and civilian volunteer.

The Enemies

World War I through the Tabloids

Because of the Zimmerman Telegram and unrestricted submarine warfare, President Wilson went before a joint session of Congress on 4 April 1917 to ask for a declaration of war. The US Senate confirmed the declared war against Germany on that day and the house confirmed it the next day. The United States did not declare war on Austria-Hungary until 7 December. The United States never declared war against the Ottoman Empire or Bulgaria.

Despite this, the emphasis was always on Germany. The focus is on the German Army, German atrocities and German Cruelty. This was in sync with British rational for the war - German invasion and violation of Belgium neutrality. While Austrians and Ottomans are seen, they play a secondary role in the war narrative.

In order to justify U.S. entry into the war, the case was made that the governments (not the people) the U.S. would be opposing, were perpetrating atrocities against innocent civilians and maintaining war. These were not democracies (like France) or Constitutional Monarchies (like Britain), but totalitarian and militaristic. By this time the Russian Monarchy was overthrown and the struggle for power in Russia was beginning.

The Germans had abandoned the spiked leather pickelhaube helmet by 1915 in favour of the steel helmet, whenever the need to invoke the brutality of the "Huns" in illustrations or propaganda the spiked helmet was trotted out.

74. Germans attacking in Belgium with gas masks and spiked helmets. This is Germans from the early war in their spiked helmets.

75. *Germans attacking in a Dutch forest in gas masks.*

76. *The German Royal Family appearing before a crowd in Berlin in 1918.*

The caption indicates that early in the war they were usually greeted with cheering and now it is more sombre.

77. The Commander of German forces around Dorpat (now Tartu, Estonia) with the name "Adams" struck the U.S. paper as humorous.

78. *The Germans being ingenious and delivering mail by airplane on the island of Oesel* (now Saaremaa, Estonia). Although some mail in different countries was being delivered by airplane, it wasn't till after the war that airplane technology was sufficient to make regular delivery of mail practical. This appears to be a Hansa-Brandenburg C1, 2-seater.

79. General von Heeringen and his staff viewing the war from an observation trench. They are using what was called a, "periscope". Josias von Heeringen (1850-1926) commanded the 7th Army until 1916 when he was transferred to Costal Command

80. Austrian prisoners captured by Italians at Figare

81. Dead Austrian cavalryman. In an era of mechanized warfare, there were still cavalry engagements on some fronts; in this case, northern Italy.

82. A Turkish prison camp showing the "dead man's line" away from the barbed wire fence.

Doughboys

World War I through the Tabloids

Doughboys was a term that was first used to describe American soldiers in the mid-19th century, but is most commonly applied to the soldiers of the World War I. It's origins are vague and is applied to each was as it was thought fit - in this case the most common reference was doughnuts. The soldiers that fought were mostly under the age of 25.

The Allies fought for three years before the US entered, by American command ignored some of the lessons learned. They also sought to keep American troops united. The Allies wanted to feed American troops into French and British units, but the President and Gen. Pershing wanted to maintain the integrity of the American Army. American readers wanted to see "their boys" in action and the pages of the press covered them in detail.

First and foremost, in the hearts and minds of the American public were the Doughboys – the American Army. Keep in mind that at this point there was only the Army and Navy as the Air force was new and just part of the aforementioned service. The army included the US marines serving in the field. Even though the navy was active in the war, particularly against u-boats, the main action was on the land and in the air.

82. *Field Battalion Entraining. Here is the latest official photographs of American boys at the front somewhere in France to reach this country. This shows an American Field Battalion entraining for a designated position with French and British troops with whom they have been brigaded in the recent fierce fight.*

This is a photo from April 1918, though it could be from the American Civil War – US troops, wagons with horses and trains

83. *An American gun crew and their field piece now in France enroute to the Lorraine trenches and other sectors where the fighting is good. No telling how many of our boys are over there, but it is a safe bet that every one of them will give a good account of himself in the great and just fight that is being waged for freeing the world from militarism and autocracy. (Committee on Public Information)*

March 1918 US forces were building up and ready for the fight on the western front. As in World War II and even though this picture reached the US sometime after the battle, unless the government wanted to point something out, locations and units were kept ambiguous.

84. *American artillery going into action in France*

Even though this was an age of increased mechanization, artillery was still moved by horses from railheads to the front lines.

World War I through the Tabloids 69

85. *An American battery in a sunken road camouflaged with farm implements, destroyed trees, bits of machinery, etc, to conceal it from enemy airmen. (French Pictorial Services)*

Concealing artillery positions in the new age of air warfare as planes could pinpoint enemy artillery for counter-battery fire.

86. (Bottom) *An American big gun being hauled into position.*

Moving from the days of field artillery that fired at visible targets, the war used cannons that fired most of the time at objectives that were not visible by the artillerymen and relied on "spotters" who relayed adjustments via signals and occasionally by field phone. It was important to call guns as "big" guns to show the might of the military arsenal. This field piece is being off loaded from a flatbed rail car at a station to move towards the front lines.

87. *The burial of Private Robert R. Bayard behind the lines in France, Chaplains Rollins and O'Connor conducting the rites.*

When Matthew Brady displayed Alexander Gardner's photographs of dead soldiers entitled, "The Dead of Antietam", the American republic was shocked by what they saw. In 1918, artillery often didn't leave much in remains. When the public was shown American dead it was either photos from life or in a setting like this where they are solemnly buried.

88. *American officers being presented to French officers of the Army of the Aisne. A very large percentage of U.S. Army officers are able to converse quite fluently in French, having made a close study of the language ever since they went into training camp. In fact, many of them already knew French before enlisting, as it is one of the requirements at West Point. French officers, on the other hand, from close affiliation for the past three years with the English, have also become quite familiar with our language, and there is, therefore, very little likelihood of confusion notwithstanding that troops of several nationalities are under one command (International Film Service)*

At the time America entered the war the French Army was the largest and most experienced of the Western Allies. From the time of Napoleon, the American Army had often looked to France as a model for the military and most "cultured" gentlemen spoke French. For the majority of American officers and troops however, it was a new experience.

89. *An American "Sky Sweeper". Portable searchlights of unusual power are now used extensively by the United States and her allies along the battlefronts. They are carried on cannon caissons; the power being generated from batteries. The photograph shows an engineer removing the cover from the drum of a 24-inch searchlight. (Committee on Public Information)*

This is an example of the changing environment of war that borders on steam punk. This is an electric light used to sweep the sky for bombers while being positioned by a horse-drawn artillery caisson. Lights were first used in the late 19th century for military operations, but during World War I these lights were used to search for enemy aircraft as well as bouncing the lights off clouds at night to create artificial light.

90. *American soldiers pause on a march*

These are anxious American troops – possibly marines based on their dark uniforms.

91. *American troops drill in a French village*

Upon their arrival in Europe, soldiers and civilians remarked on the height and health of US troops. Gen Pershing made sure his lean troops were effectively drill and the media was happy to show them doing it.

92. *American soldiers who are acting as military police in Paris drawn up for review. Together with the American air squadron these men do invaluable service in preserving order and safety in the French capital (Committee on Public Information)*

Paris was the objective of any American soldiers on leave. They had money, access to rationed food and loved to raise hell. When the caption says "preserving order" that was as much for American troops as their allied counter-parts.

World War I through the Tabloids

93. *This photograph which has just arrived in this country shows American infantry marching through a French village on their way to the front. The American forces have already won the commendation of the French for their great chivalry and undaunted courage. (Underwood & Underwood)*

A running commentary in the US papers was the bravery of US troops. While allied troops had cautious experience after several years of war, the Americans had enthusiasm and something to prove which sometimes resulted in unneeded casualties. American doughboys initially would not need the advice of the veteran soldiers and eventually developed their own pace to the war.

94. *Grewsome (sic) souvenirs of the Huns' hate: flame projectors brought back by our boys after a raid on the Boche trenches in March. Though liquid fire is forbidden by the rules of warfare, the Germans use it freely. (Committee on Public Information)*

The first practical flamethrowers in the modern era were adopted by the German Army in 1901. They were first used by the Germans in 1915. Despite the statement in the press above that "Though forbidden by the rules of warfare..." the British Army had been using them since 1916. They were used against American troops such as the "Lost Battalion", but were dangerous to the users as well as the defenders.

95. *Resting After A Hard Battle. Do you know any of them? All those boys proved themselves American heroes against the Germans at the battle of Cantigny for the daring way they stemmed the repeated assaults made against them by the enemy. The British and French troops said they went into the fray like veterans or war and showered (sic) all kinds of praise on them. (Committee on Public Information)*

The Battle of Cantigny, fought May 28, 1918 was the first major American battle and offensive of World War I. The U.S. 1st Division, the most experienced of the five American divisions then in France and in reserve for the French Army near the village of Cantigny, was selected for the attack. The objective of the attack was both to reduce a small salient made by the German Army in the front lines but also to instill confidence among the French and British allies in the ability of the inexperienced American Expeditionary Force (AEF).

96. *HEROIC OFFICERS BEING DECORATED AT BUCKINGHAM. Wounded British officers are shown in this photograph being received and invested with the D.S.O. and badges of knighthood in the quadrangle of Buckingham Palace. To the right are the royal apartments protected by heavy wire netting, which is stretched above the roof of the royal residence. A British airship, a "sausage," is seen patrolling above the palace, a unit of an aerial force that is ever on watch for raiders. King George is shown at the right pinning a medal to the breast of a hero.*

As part of the effort to promote American efforts in the War and because soldiers were often operationally joined with troops of foreign countries, American soldiers sometimes were nominated for foreign medals for heroism such as the "Croix de Guerre" and the "Distinguished Service Order". This was a source of pride for American troops and people on the home front

97. *American soldiers marching in London.*

Unlike World War II where England was a major staging area for American forces, England was not a major hub of American forces. None-the-less some of Uncle Sam's boys trained there before heading to the front. These doughboys were wearing the campaign hat rather than the rakish fore-and-aft cap.

America at War

98. *American soldiers in London meeting the Lord Mayor*

American forces introduced to the Lord Mayor of London – Horace Brook Marshall. Marshall was an influential newspaper publisher.

99. *Americans resting in a French cemetery during the battle at Picardy.*

Although the caption lists these boys as Americans during the battle of Picardy (8-12 August 1918), that action involved primarily British, French, Canadian and Australian troops.

100. *American and French officers watching a German Taube over our lines – At the top in the winter trenches (Committee on Public Information)*

The use of the word "Taube" (Dove) was a nickname early in the war for German airplanes. The top picture must have been early in 1918 with snow on the ground.

78   America at War

101. *An American regiment receives its battle flags on the Picardy Front*

At the beginning of the war in 1914 some units may have carried flags into battle, but by 1918 when this photo was taken, battle flags were a ceremonial item that remained with the regiment's HQ.

102. *Scene at the first baseball game in the Bois de Boulogne between the American Army and Navy in Paris taking keen interest in the sport. Families in Paris, on the sidelines with puckered brows tying to figure out what this American National Game is all about anyway.*

Professional sports was an outcome of more leisure time. Watching sports went hand in hand with that. Baseball was one of the few professional sports and popular with American troops. To Europeans it was a curiosity.

103. *Baseball between the Army and Navy in France*

Americans played baseball where they could, when they could in France. You'll notice the crowd standing close to the players along the foul line. It was not unusual in the US, as well as France to have spectators line the field and the outfield in crowded games. Notice the large handle bat in use.

104. *Admiral Sims displays top-season form, pitches the first ball in a game between U.S. Army and Navy teams at Highbury, England. After the Admiral had gone to the bench, however, the Army won. The Canadians in the bleachers, seem only mildly interested.*

Unlike the game above in France, this game in England seems to have been played at a regular sports field with the players in baseball uniforms. William Sims was the commander of US naval forces in Europe during World War I. Sims career spanned the 19th and 20th century and was instrumental in helping to modernize the navy.

105. *Capt. Martin H. Meany of the 165th, formerly of the 69th New York, wounded recently, is just 26 years old.*

The ability to place photographs in publications allowed newspapers to identify local individuals. The 69th New York is one of the famous New York regiments with a long history. From a New York Times obituary, 2 June 1970) Martin H. Meaney, survived the war becoming deputy police commissioner and a retired Army brigadier general, before dying in 1970. He was 81 years old and lived at 1224 East 32d Street in the Flatbush section of Brooklyn. Mr. Meaney retired from the Police Department in 1958, after having supervised the department's administrative affairs as Fifth Deputy Commissioner for 25 years. He saw action in three conflicts, first as a private at the Mexican border in 1916. In France with the old Fighting 69th in World War I, Mr. Meaney was gassed and twice wounded. He emerged as a major at the war's end. He was the regiment's executive officer in Europe during World War I, and served in the Pacific with the 27th Division, in World War II. After moving into Italy with the Allied Military Government in 1943, he headed the country's civilian police for a time. He returned to his desk at Manhattan police headquarters in 1945.

106. *The casino at Aix-les-Bains, France, where great numbers of American soldiers spend their leave. Several of the men are playing checkers, while the rest are looking on and at the same time posing for this photograph. It will be noticed that at least two of the boys are wearing decorations. Every branch of the service is represented in this group and the experiences of many are no doubt very thrilling. (International Film Service).*

The casino Grand-Cercle is located in France in the municipality of Aix-les-Bains, in the Savoy region. The Grand-Cercle Casino was built by King Victor Emmanuel II of Savoy in 1850. It was designed by a Chambéry architect Charles-Bernard Pellegrini. The building at the time included in its central part a ballroom flanked by two lounges, one for gaming, the other for reading and correspondence. Thirty years later, the Casino was expanded with two side pavilions. In 1899, the building acquired a theater with 900 seats, equipped with wooden machinery. At the start of World War I it was used for a convalescent center and eventually a hospital with an operating room. In 1916 it became a receiving center for soldiers on leave.

World War I through the Tabloids

107. *Lieut. John David of Dillon, S.C. and Pershing's army, died gloriously on the field of battle in France after killing seven Huns. (International Film)*

According to The Greenville Daily News, "First Lieut. John Hodges David, Jr., whose name appeared in the casualty list given out by Gen. Pershing Monday, is the first South Carolina officer to lose his life in action and the first Furman University man to be killed since the entrance of the United States into the war." David was from Dillon and graduated from the Citadel in the class of 1914. He was commissioned as a first lieutenant following his graduation from the first Fort Oglethorpe training camp and volunteered for service in France. Lieutenant David was the son of Dr. and Mrs. J.H. David of Dillon. "Though no details of the death of Lieut. David were given out, it is thought that he was killed when a squad of twenty-seven men charging over No Man's Land several days ago was wiped out. Lieut. David may have been in command of the raiding party which unexpectedly clashed with a German patrol." – Source: The Greenville Daily News, 14 Mar. 1918, p.2.

108. *This is the distinguished service cross of the United States, the new decoration granted for exceptional bravery in battle. (Committee on Public Information)*

Prior to the Medal of Honor, which was created in 1861, the US military forces did not award medals as was done in many European armies. Occasionally special silver medals were awarded to individuals. According to the code of regulations, The Distinguished Service Cross was established by President Woodrow Wilson on January 2, 1918. General Pershing recommended that another medal other than the Medal of Honor be authorized for the Armed Forces of the United States for valorous service rendered in like manner to that awarded by the European Armies. The request for establishment of the medal was forwarded from the Secretary of War to the President in a letter dated 28 December 1917. The Act of Congress establishing this award (193-65th Congress), dated 9 July 1918, is contained in 10 U.S.C. § 3742. The establishment of the Distinguished Service Cross was promulgated in War Department General Order No. 6, dated 12 January 12, 1918. The Distinguished Service Cross was originally designed by J. Andre Smith, an artist employed by the United States Army during World War I and manufactured by the United States Mint at Philadelphia, Pennsylvania. The die was cast from the approved design prepared by Captain Aymar E. Embury II, Engineers Officer Reserve Corps. Upon examination of the first medals struck at the Mint, it was considered advisable to make certain minor changes to add to the beauty and the attractiveness of the medal. Due to the importance of the time element involved in furnishing the decorations to Gen Pershing, one hundred of the medals were struck from the original design. These medals were furnished with the provision that these crosses be replaced when the supply of the second design was accomplished.

109. *PART OF THEIR "BAG" – These doughty doughboys are wearing German hats and are displaying their souvenirs captured by the Americans when they routed the Germans at the battle of Seicheprey. Among the other trophies in the picture may be seen a Boche gun, gas mask, wire cutter and canteen. (Committee on Public Information)*

The American Expeditionary Forces fought one of its earliest World War I engagements at the tiny hamlet of Seicheprey, France on April 20, 1918. Seicheprey lay on the southern edge of the St. Mihiel salient, a deep 25 mile bulge pointing west into the Allied lines. Seicheprey was a surprise battle as far as the Americans were concerned. They weren't expecting a fight when the Germans struck at them from the north in the wee hours of the morning. In front of the Germans was the US 26th Infantry Division, which along with the 1st, 2nd and 42nd Infantry Divisions, was one of the first four American divisions to reach France. US troops posed with a pile of booty reinforces the idea that the allies were successful in the field.

110. *Clad in his official robes, the Mayor personally greets the officers of the detachment. The men are to undergo training for the front at a cantonment nearby. After a few months they will be moved to France and gradually will be sent into action (Western Newspaper Union)*

The Lord Mayor was a recognizable and accessible figure when it came to meetings with US troops

World War I through the Tabloids 83

111. *American soldiers in the Aisne region, near the scene of the great battle and ready to do their part when called, form in line for the noon mess and drop on the ground to eat the hot food from the field kitchens. (Kadel & Herbert)*

Feeding troops in the field has long been a problem for armies. The use of field kitchens afforded troops hot meals – all troops would still complain about the quality of food in all armies. Still, it was better than the hard crackers (hardtack) and bully beef (canned beef akin to spam). It was not until World War II that K-rations were finally developed for troops in the line.

112. *Officers leading a regiment of American infantry to the front line for duty in the trenches on the sector held by our men. Notice what a husky lot they are. (Committee on Public Information)*

Articles and photographs emphasize how much bigger and stronger US forces were compare to their European counterparts.

America at War

113. Marines in Action

The US Marines made a name for themselves in the fighting on the western front, especially in the fighting at Belleau Wood in May 1918. This drawing shows Marines shooting a Hotchkiss Mle14 medium machine gun, a versatile weapon used up to the 1960's. US forces used more than 7,000 of these during the war.

114. *Baseball is in the fiber of American boys as French instructors are amazed at the accuracy of these Marines in grenade practice*

World War I through the Tabloids 85

115. *A detachment of General Pershing's army resting on the march to reinforce the French and English in Picardy (French Official Photograph)*

These doughboys are in complete gear including the 1903 gear which had a long cylindrical backpack, an example of which is below.

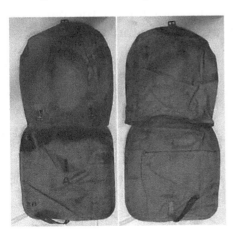

116. *This is one of the first photos to reach this country showing American soldiers being decorated by the French on the western front. General Debeny, commander of a French Army Corps, is pinning the Croix de Guerre on one of the Yankee heroes. Detachments of American troops from the battalion that repelled the raid of March 1, in which these heroes distinguished themselves are seen in the background. Premier Clemenceau attended the ceremonies. He is seen at the left with a group of officers. Stories of American valor are becoming more plentiful as the opportunities for dash and daring are presented. (Underwood and Underwood)*

As with the picture above with the King of England, American soldiers are shown winning medals from foreign powers, showing their bravery in the fight against oppression

117. *Another photograph of U.S. soldiers at Aix-les-Bains, the rest center of the American fighting forces in France. This shows a number of men ready to depart for the firing line after a happy furlough (International Film)*

Aik-les-Bains is a town in Southeastern France near the Swiss-Italian border on the bank of Lac du Bourget, away from most of the fighting.

World War I through the Tabloids

118. Post cards like this were often sent home to let folks know they were ok. This dispatch rider has chains on the tires of his motorcycle to cover rough roads.

On the Eastern Front

By the time the U.S. entered the war, the Russians were on their way out. The Tsar abdicated in March 1917 and the United States Congress declared war in April. By 1918 the first phase of the Russian Revolution was over, Russia was out of the war and the Civil War was in going strong. In March 1918 the Brest-Litovsk peace treaty had taken Russia completely out of the war. In April 1918, the Germans landed troops in Finland which forced the allies to send troops to Northwestern Russia around Murmansk. By August 1918 allied troops were in Vladivostok protecting war material from falling into Soviet hands.

At the same time that Russia was disintegrating new/old countries were appearing. Although some were created as satellite states by Germany, they were still viewed by American newspapers as loyal allies. In April 1918 in the wake of Brest-Litovsk, the Hetmanate was established as a modern Ukrainian state to combat the Soviet government, Poland, Lithuania and the Baltic states were being set-up as independent entities.

119. This photograph was originally of the Petrograd demonstrations in July 1917. This was re-used to condemn the "Soviets and anarchists". "Bolsheviks and Anarchists who propose to set up disorder in place of such order as the world has been able to maintain condemn themselves and their system" (International Film Service)

90   America at War

120. *"Minimum Comfort at Maximum Cost". The next time you start to complain about wartime railroad traveling inconveniences, count to ten and think of this picture. Here is an example of minimum comfort at maximum cost – private car rates for box car accommodation. Remember, that no matter how unsatisfactory rail travel is at the present time, it can never become as intolerable as it is in Russia. These British soldiers had to wait eight days before they could find a railroad car to take them to Petrograd. And they were charged $75 each for the privilege of riding in this box car. But with characteristic philosophy – and with the $75 each in mind – they chalked the name of London's best hotel on the side of the car. They were photographed on their arrival in Petrograd."* Note the bucket used for washing up. (International)

The British force in northern Russia faced problems from the Germans, Soviets and evidently rail transport as well. With a nod to scenes from Dr. Zhivago. The boxcar says, "Cecil Hotel" Wagon Occupied. By comparison, you could travel across the United States in 1918 with a sleeper birth for $75

121. *A photo of the Ukrainian peace signed in February 1918.*

This was the first "Brest-Litovsk Treaty" signed solely with the Ukraine when Russia balked. It prompted Trotsky to declare, "No war – no peace". The Germans had used the Soviet proclamation of self-determination to declare the Baltic states, Russian Poland and the Ukraine independent at different times. The caption reads "Photograph taken at a meeting the night of February 9, when the Ukrainians signed the German peace terms. Those seated at the table are Count Czernin, von Kuchlmann, Talaat Pasha, General Hoffman, H. Lewytsky and M. Radaslovof, the two later being the Ukrainian delegates." (International Film Service) Richard von Kühlmann was the German Foreign Secretary, Gen. Max Hoffmann was the German Chief of Staff for the Eastern Front, Count Ottokar

Czernin was the Austrian Foreign Minister and Talaat Pasha represented Turkey. The spelling of these names lacked consistency in the papers.

122. *Officers of the new Ukrainian Hetmanate.*

Following the collapse of the Tsarist Regime, Ukrainians in the former Russian Empire declared independence and established the Ukrainian National Republic. The Kaiser's government, eager to send the German troops currently serving on the Eastern Front toward Paris, pressured Lenin and Trotsky to end the war by signing a peace treaty. The Soviets, waiting for a proletarian revolution to sweep Germany, refused to sign. To gain political leverage over the Soviets, on 9 February 1918 the Germans signed the First Treaty of Brest-Litowsk with the Ukrainian National Republic. In the Treaty, the Germans pledged to provide military aid to Ukraine in their struggle against the Bolsheviks while in turn the Ukrainian government would deliver large quantities of foodstuffs to the Central Powers.

The Germans, unhappy with the social-democratic orientation of the Ukrainian National Republic, supported a change in the Ukrainian government. Their choice was a conservative landowner Pavlo Skoropadskyi who focused on law and order. To protect the new regime, the Germans and Austrians allowed for the recruitment of ethnic Ukrainians held in their POW camps. In order to provide a visible historical legitimacy to the new regime, the men's uniforms mimicked traditional Cossack dress. Impressive mustaches, such as the ones pictured here, were the rage at the time.

123. *"The Kaiser last month graciously bestowed 'independence' on Lithuania. These pictures come direct from Holzminden, Germany, and show groups of Lithuanian children, in a war prisoners' camp, absolutely free except for the barbed wire in the background (in the top picture) and (below) learning from German teachers what a good German Shakespeare was."*

Germany established a Lithuanian Republic in February 1918. There was a cynical acknowledgment of it in the press. The establishment of an independent Lithuania was established in the same agreement that established an independent Ukraine. In January 1917 Germany declared they would create a Polish Kingdom based on the Russian areas captured in 1914-1917. In March 1918 they declared a native Civil Administration for Poland, Lithuania and Kurland (Latvia).

124. *"A machine gun company of the White Guard of Finland, which recently crushed the Red Guard (Bolsheviki) army captured the city of Viborg"* (Central News)

On 29 April 1918 the White Guards recaptured Viborg from the Red Guards where it remained under Finnish control until the Russo-Finish War of 1940.

Propaganda

World War One was not the first war to use propaganda for friends and foes, but it was just as much a part of the war as those fought in the trenches. While the U.S. was neutral until 1917, the press for the most part feed off of Allied news stories. The Germans might release a photo of many allied prisoners as a sign that they were winning, but it would be interpreted that they were not properly taking care of prisoners.

Stories of German atrocities starting in Belgium and continuing in France were common occurrences prior to the U.S. entry into the war, and were continued after the U.S. entry. In an age of limited media access and the inability to fact-check, these stories were often the only real filter for news reaching the American people.

In the Allied press, towns and villages full of innocent people were shown as foibles of German military cruelty and supported the need for U.S. involvement in the conflict. Some of these charges were real, some were exaggerated, and some were made up.

125. *Executions in Serbia – The horrors of Belgium are being reproduced in Serbia where the Austrians appear anxious to exceed their German allies' ferocity against people of conquered territories. The Austrians seem determined to wipe out entire inhabitants of conquered districts of Serbia. They are not satisfied with wreaking their vengeance on soldiers and practically starving the entire civilian population, but on the flimsiest excuses have hung many non-combatants. This photo smuggled into Switzerland by an escaped Serb is the first picture of this phase of the atrocities to reach the United States. It is a typical scene of innocent civilians hanging on roadside gibbets (Underwood & Underwood).*

From the early days of the war there were reports of atrocities directed against the civilian populations of occupied countries. This was especially true in Belgium but was carried over elsewhere. Austrian retaliation against Serbs and the Turks in Armenia were real issues but they wee not new to war.

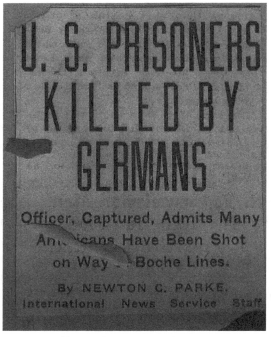

126. *Headline of Germans killing American prisoners (top left)*

There were instances of men killed during surrender. Early in the war, especially, violence was reported against French prisoners. Both sides accepted that this would happen, but eventually tried to stop it.[1] This may or may not have happened, but the US public would willingly accept it.

127. *Germans kill British prisoners (top right)*

The German military routinely used POW's in construction and work details that sometimes put them near fighting. Officers were generally spared from this activity.

128. *German's abusing British prisoners in the early war.*

The guards are wearing a version of the pickelhaube, by this time in the war (1918) they would not have worn this helmet but were easily identifiable by it. This was most likely a drawing from early in the war that was re-used by the press.

---

[1] Brian K. Feltman. "Tolerance as a crime? The British treatment of German prisoners of war on the Western Front, 1914-1918", *War in History* 17/4, 2010, pp. 435-458.

World War I through the Tabloids

German Airmen Bomb Refugees Fleeing on French Roads

By International News Service.
PARIS, June 5.—German airmen, flying over the roads leading from the Marne battle front, are dropping bombs and firing with machine guns upon the crowds of refugees fleeing from the scene of the fighting.

Many civilians have fallen victims to this new phase of brutality.

Refugees from the invaded districts continue to pour into Paris and unfold tales of horror. They declare that the Uhlans ejected all the villagers from occupied territory, refusing to take any prisoners. The fugitive swarms are made up of old men and women and children.

129. *Germans making war on civilians.*

In June 1918 the Germans were pushing toward the Marne again in an offensive. In the wake of this long lines of civilians sought refuge in Paris and away from the advancing Germans. It is possible, but unlikely that German planes attacked civilians.

130. *Victim of German "Kultur" – Here is one more reason for a "peace with victory". It is the funeral procession which carried the body of Mlle. Lere, a French nurse, to her grave. The woman was killed in the bombardment of a day nursery near Paris by one of the German long-range guns. The women in the picture are nurse who were friends of the dead woman. There were other innocent victims of the bombardment. (Underwood & Underwood)*

The Hague Convention of 1907 prohibited naval bombardment against undefended coastal towns, but cities that were being defended were subject to bombardment. The power of guns meant that they could shoot from long distance without a real sense of where it would land. Civilian casualties were acceptable if they occurred as a by-product of war. This was viewed as negligent

131. *British soldiers found a French child abandoned or forgotten in the flight from the Germans. They took it with them to a barn where they placed it for warmth and safety between them. In the night a German bomb fell the barn killing both men, but the child was found asleep and unharmed.*

Human interest stories of soldiers saving civilians were meant to tug on the heart strings of American readers.

132. *French flags waved in this street in Alsace as the crowd went home from church. Ten minutes later the Germans came.*

This picture was taken during the Spring Offensive of 1918 but reinforced the patriotism of the French occupied by the Germans.

133. *The arrival in Paris of the first refugees from the towns overrun by the Germans in the Great Drive. Most of them escaped with only their personal belongings. All were treated sympathetically and provided food and shelter.*

As in image 132 civilians sought to escape from the front lines by moving toward Paris. The Germans were happy to allow this as the extra civilians would have put an added strain the economy and food supplies. The government had to accept them, but then find places for them to stay.

134. *Children displaced by the German Advance are treated by French soldiers*

This disruption and displacement of children was the most difficult part of war. Presents and new clothes did not totally make up for the disruption of their lives, but according to this photo it did seem to take some of the sting out.

135. *Another German military coup. Throngs of children forced to leave Paris to escape air raids.*

In October a mutiny of sailors at Kiel was set off by Officers who tried to set sail into battle on their own initiative. The follow-up to refugees coming into Paris is that air raids and big guns eventually forced them to leave.

136. "Bobbies who have been released from the London Police force for military service in France, marching away to don their new uniforms and begin life in the army. (Committee on Public Information)

As the war dragged on for four years more and more in the UK, men were needed to fill the ranks. Some jobs and personnel who might have been exempt in the first few years were called upon to serve in the line. This was the case with the London Policemen pictured here.

102   America at War

Figure 137. *A line of headlines*

Small articles continued to promote atrocities every day, some outrageous, (Enemy Crucifies Two Americans) hammering home atrocities against civilians, yet only a small article about a new decoration for valor – The Distinguished Service Cross.

The Distinguished Service Cross was requested by President Wilson in January 1918 and established by the Act of July 1918. General Pershing had requested the establishment of this award when the Medal of Honor did not apply.

138. *Figure of Christ still intact in church at Breelen, which were wrecked by German guns. (British Pictorial Service)*

The destruction of a church was again seen as a desecration needlessly done by German guns.

WHAT ENEMY HIGH EXPLOSIVE SHELL DID TO A FRENCH HOME

139. *Few photographs of the Great War have furnished more action to the square inch than the one produced herewith. A powerful shell has just exploded in the group of buildings in the background wrecking them and strewing the surrounding territory with debris. That the photographer was "on the job" when the explosion occurred is evidenced by the smoke and dust arising from the wreckage. The Tommy seen in the foreground jumped out of the shelter just in time to get into the picture. (Underwood & Underwood)*

Photographers and newsreels tried to give the "feel" of war. To most people this was still gallant men charging across battlefields – like the American troops attempted after the veteran armies stopped this. The destruction that war was capable on inflicting on was not fully transformed to the home front.

140. *Gathering the little orphans of war from the ruins of their homes – these Sisters of Mercy in an Italian village rescuing the bewildered little ones after a bombardment by the Austrians – fathers fighting in the army and mothers the victims.*

If the horrors of war visited upon soldiers could not be comprehended, the effects upon children could sometimes be more powerful

141. *Refugees fleeing before the Germans, enter suburbs of Paris. Note the baby forced to walk with the rest of the family.*

More refugees entering Paris before being sent to other points. Old women in carts and children on foot.

142. *Stricken Rheims is the forefront of the public interest again. Once more with the Teutonic Hordes at her gate, she is on fire.*

Once again civilian towns destroyed by the Germans

143. Robert College was founded in Istanbul, Turkey, by Dr. Cyrus Hamlin, an educator, inventor, technician, architect and builder, and Mr. Christopher Rheinlander Robert, a well-known philanthropist and a wealthy merchant from New York. Is now Bogazici University. It was and still is an English language university for foreigners in Istanbul. There was an attempted to use the US professors at the University as propaganda to gain US support for the Central Powers.

144. *When the French troops sent aid to the Italians against the Teutons passed through Solferino on their way to the front, they stopped at the famous ossuary to pay their respects to the members of the French soldiers who died facing the Austrians June 24, 1859. This photo shows a corner of the ossuary and a cabinet of skulls (Underwood)*

The Battle of Solferino was the largest battle since Leipzig in 1813 with over 300,000 soldiers involved. It was also the last time ruling monarchs led troops into battle as Napoleon III, Victor Emmanuel II and Franz Joseph all commanded their respective armies. The battle lasted over nine hours and while each side lost only 2,100 men killed, the horror of it moved Napoleon III to make peace. It also influenced the formation of the Red Cross

The use of prisoners for propaganda purposes worked two ways – either showing how well one side was doing or how inhumanely they were treated.

145. *Allied prisoners arrive at German camps*

These soldiers seem to be wearing Russian style uniforms. This could either be a photo from earlier in the war or Romanian troops in 1918

146. *The interior of a German camp. This picture and others are the types of photographs which the German Government sent to this country before we entered the war, after they had been dialed up to create a favourable impression. (Brown Brothers)*

Allied prisoners had a mixed existence in German prison camps. Enlisted men were often used in construction projects, exposed to the elements and artillery fire. As the war went on Germany suffered from food shortages caused by the allied blockade and four years war which caused starvation and lack of basic items in camps.

147. *Soup lines at Zossen: Another misleading German propaganda photograph (Henry Ruschin)*

Zossen is a town near Berlin that was the site of a German garrison and several prisoner of war camps including the "Crescent Camp" for Muslim soldiers in the allied armies that included a wooden mosque.

148. *Russian prisoners in a prison camp in Germany (Henry Ruschin)*

Another shot of a large group of Russians in a camp with canvas buildings. Russian troops captured by the Germans particularly suffered from overcrowding and lack of basic elements.

149. *Remarkable photograph of an internment camp for French prisoners near Wuerztburg, Bavaria, showing heavy field guns in position on huge mounds commanding the encampment, ready for instant operation if the prisoners should make a concerted effort to break bounds. On the right can be seen an observation box, also overlooking the encampment. From a photograph brought to Paris by a French prisoner who recently escaped. (Underwood & Underwood)*

Escaping from prisoner of war camps in Germany was not an easy thing. The camps were deep in Germany and the prisoners had little knowledge of the countryside. Charles De Gaulle made five unsuccessful attempts to escape after he was captured

150. *A scene on the Somme Battlefield showing a detachment of French cavalryman bring in a big batch of German prisoners. Two of the fiercest battles of the war have been fought in this region. St Quentin, Peronne and Amiens are important cities on the Somme. (Photo International Film Service)*

The Allied papers used examples like these to show how the Allies were "winning".

World War I through the Tabloids 111

151. *A group of German prisoners captured in the dugouts and amid the wreckage of the German first line of trenches. Almost without exception the boches give themselves up with great cheerfulness whenever the opportunity offers, knowing that they will be well feed and kindly treated. (Kadel & Herbert)*

By July and August 1918, the German army was starting to lose the will to fight but were still dangerous enemies. The copy line did make a point of saying how the enemy would be treated fair and fed.

152. *These are types of German soldiers, many of the thousands by the Allies during the desperate Teutonic thrusts in Picardy. That Germany is hard pressed for manpower can be easily seen by the extremes in ages of the captured soldier; bearded middle-aged men and boys barely out of their teens. The slenderness of the captives plainly advertises the scantiness of the nourishment in the Land of the Kaiser. It will be noticed that the captives are wearing flimsy leggings (instead of boots). (International)*

There is a great deal of truth to this photo as Germany was calling up older and younger men as a whole generation of men were already under arms. This was a reason the entry of the U.S. into the way had such a profound effect – while the European powers bled themselves dry a new pool of soldiers were coming from across the Atlantic.

153. *AND THEY ARE STILL COMING. Every time the Kaiser tries to break through the Allied lines on his "way" to the coast or Paris, General Foch has to brush union rules aside and work his artisan reserves overtime building new prison pens and camps for captured subjects of His Teutonic Majesty. Until the final numbers can be cast up and tabulated, there is no way of knowing just how many prisoners have poured back to these improvised detention pens to during the last few months. Here is only one small cluster of the many that dot the country to the north of the French capital. (International)*

Prisoners always seem to be lined up by barbed wire fences.

154. *German prisoners in UK*

These German prisoners may have been in captivity for some time. You can see that several have traded their uniform items for civilian clothes

155. *The great offensive was all one-sided even in the beginning, as witnessed this group of Germans captured by the British in the Montdidier region early in the fray.*

These are Germans captured in the Second Somme. Two of the British cavalrymen are keeping the prisoners in line with lances

The Wounded

    The idea of battlefield triage was developed in the First World War. Soldiers that were wounded at the front were first taken to a series of different areas to treat their injuries. This started in the line with litter bearers to aid stations. From there they could be sent to dressing stations. Those in need were then sent by ambulances to field hospitals. The next step was evacuation hospitals or convalescent depots. Those in need or further help were sent to a regulating stations to forward to Advance Base Hospitals or Base Hospitals.
    Doctors not only had to deal with the trauma of more efficient killing weapons, but the effects of different types of gas which had short and long-term effects.

During the American Civil War, photographers took photographs of American wounded and dead, but these were only shown in special exhibitions such as "The Dead of Antietam". The papers would show American wounded, but tended to be either being treated or smiling after treatment. Although photos were taken of wounded soldiers, these were not shown to the public.

Better medical treatment and technology, also meant that men who were disfigured would survive, but needed to be able to function back in society. Plastic surgery was still in its infancy, but the Cambridge Military Hospital at Aldershot pioneered the process. The upshot was that people at home were encouraged that war wounds could be healed or disguised.

156. *Tending the Wounded Under Fire. A trench dressing station along the British battle front, showing Canadian stretcher bearers giving first aide to the wounded during the course of a German assault. The two men standing against the walls at the left are wearing tags to describe the nature of their injuries. (Canadian War Office)*

This is the beginning of modern military medicine where the neediest are sent first.

157. *British wounded on the Flanders battlefield about to start for England on the Red Cross train. The real meaning of blighty is shown on their faces and the gestures of their comrades who are seeing them off. (Official Canadian War Official Photo)*

"Blighty" is a slang term for Britain. The soldier on the right with the white armband has the initials "SB" in it for "stretcher-bearer."

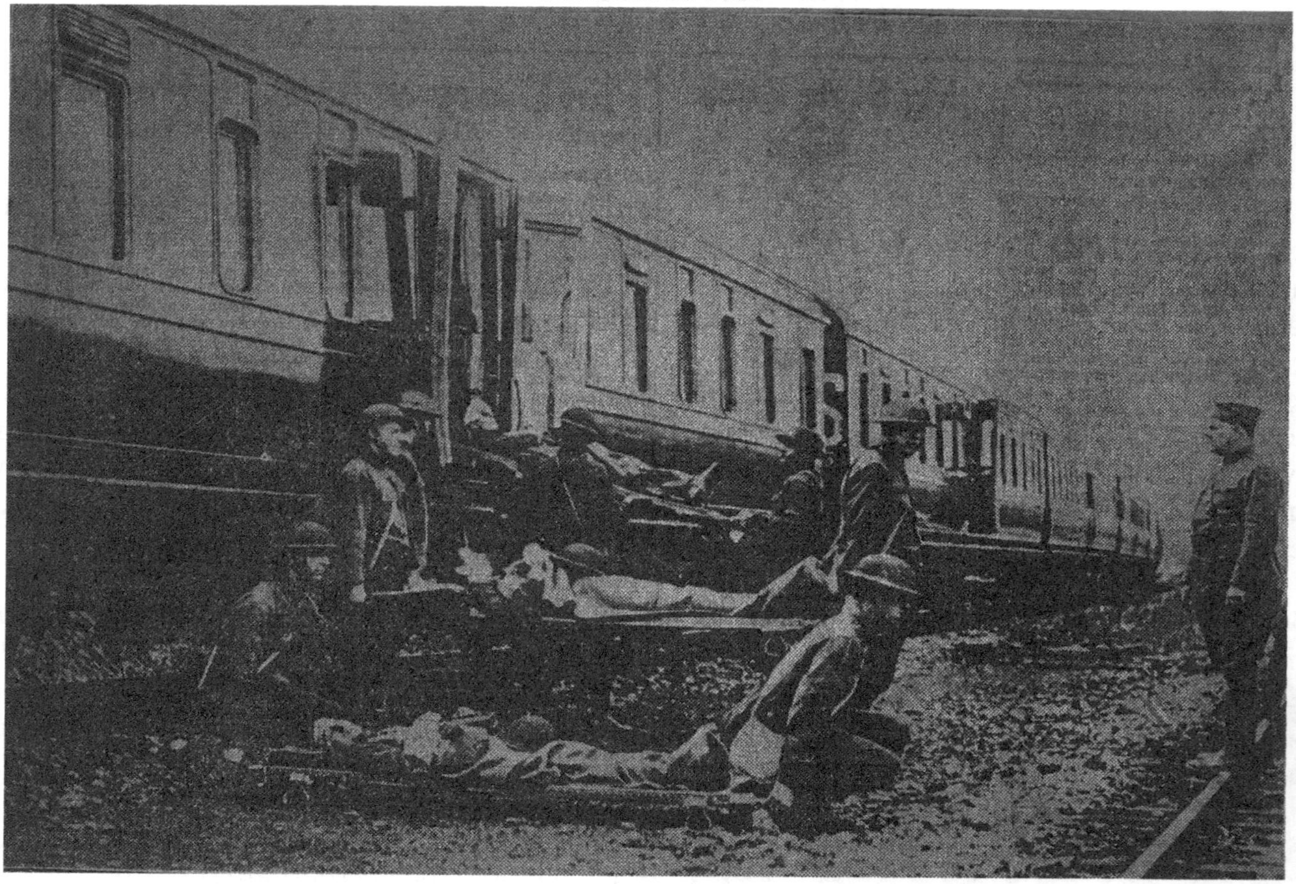

158. *American wounded awaiting transportation on a hospital train. One wounded soldier is being lifted into the hospital train in France while two other waiting on stretchers to be put on board. (Committee on Public Information from Underwood & Underwood)*

American wounded made their way through a series of aid stations from the front lines to hospitals in Paris.

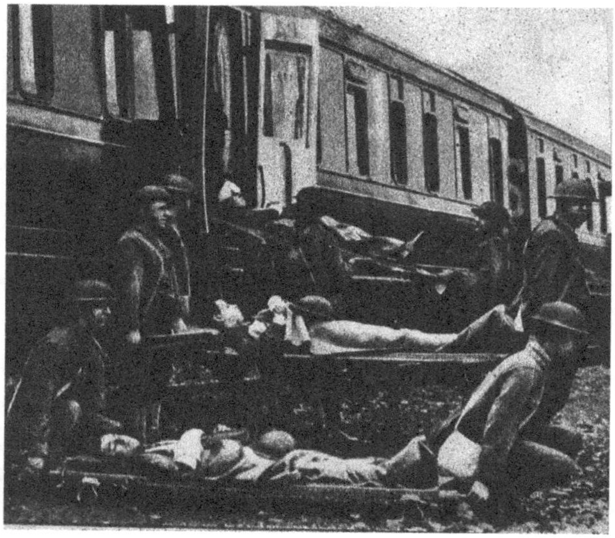

159. *Stretcher bearers placing wounded, who have already received first aid, on an American Hospital train for transportation to permanent hospitals.*

The previous photo re-used here in another publication but focused on one section and provides more detail.

World War I through the Tabloids

117

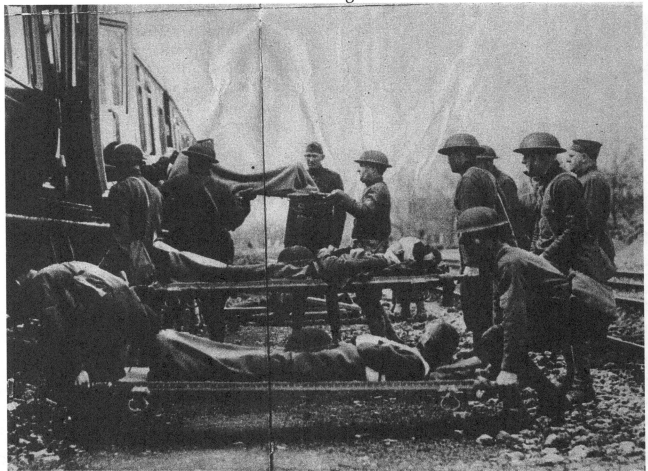

160. *These pictures are the first to show how our wounded are handled in France and how they comfort themselves under the painful circumstances. At the left the convalescent is reading the "Stars and Stripes", the soldier's paper. Above, wounded are being put on the train and on the right some of them are shown in the car talking with the surgeons. Don't they look cheerful and courageous in their misfortunes.* (Committee on Public Information)

This is a follow-up photo from the two previous one's involving loading the wounded onto the train. *Stars and Stripes* was fist published by veteran newspaper men in the AEF from 8 February 1918 to 13 June 1919. After they returned home several would go on to found *The New Yorker* magazine. It was an eight-page weekly format that reached over 500,000 readers in France. During World War II it was printed in several editions across multiple theaters of war.

161. The Interior of the train with wounded soldiers. Despite some of their "wounds" they seem to be nonchalantly reading. These trains were specially outfitted to have upper and lower areas to lay stretchers or soldiers.

162. *Here is shown a wounded British Tommy who has helped to hold back the German offensive. The British have had a strenuous time, at one point there were only fourteen divisions against forty-eight enemy divisions and at another, seventy-five German divisions opposed two British armies. Note the inveterate cigarette in the wounded man's mouth, which apparently, he is enjoying to the utmost. (British Official Photo from Underwood & Underwood).*

Packaged cigarettes had just started to gain popularity in the early 1900's with brands such as "Camel" in the US. They were handed out to soldiers for a variety of reasons.

163. *The Captured Helmet. Red Cross workers brought in a Canadian soldier so badly wounded he was nearly unconscious; but through his hours of anguish he clutched firmly a German helmet that he captured in the fight that nearly cost him his life. This news photo inspired staff poet Edmund Vance Cooke to the following lines:*

This is my trophy and I hold it fast;
    It is a Kaiser-creature's outer shell;
I brought it through the hot and hideous blast
    Which gushes from the middle lakes of hell.
Yet think it not a pretty pride in me,
    Or this the guerdon of some sudden brawl,
But that I struck my blow to hold me free
    And felled not my foe, but the foe of all.
I slew him not for alien tongue or birth,
    Or any hatred of him in my veins;
I slew him because his banner fouled the earth
    And threatened babies unborn with hate and chains.
      - Edmund Vance Cooke

War trophies were prized by many men. Even the wounded. World War I for some reason inspired collecting trophies of war. Edmund Vance Cooke was a Canadian-American poet (1866 – 1932) who was known for reading poems over the radio.

164. *Its hard for a wounded soldier to find much humor in life, but the fact that he is riding back to the base hospital on the shoulders of four captured Huns tickled this Tommy's funny bone. The Germans can't seem to see the joke at all.*

Whimsy and humor also figure prominently into themes. Here the enemy who created the issue, help carry the wounded.

World War I through the Tabloids

165. *Two of the American first American wounded in France, Charles Geigner of Chicago, Il at the left, and E. Darland of Petersburg, IL at the right. The latter an engineer fought at Cambrai. Both look cheerful despite the loss of limbs. (Wyndham Press Service, from International Film)*

Americans in Paris. May have lost a limb, but never their dash. This breaks the mold of showing wounded US soldiers.

166. Prosthetic masks offered hope for those maimed in battle. This was the beginning of the development of plastic surgery, but for many soldiers maimed in combat, prosthetic pieces were a way to hide the injuries to the flesh.

167. *Brothers in Arms. (British Official Photo, Underwood & Underwood). Wounded British soldiers shown helping their wounded comrades. This photograph was taken just behind the enemy lines.*

British soldiers helping a wounded comrade from the front. The tags hanging off them indicates the type of injury they have received.

Incidents of War

For people at the home front it was not just the war itself that interested them, but the lives of the men fighting there. For soldiers and observers a sense of normalcy in abnormal times was important. To that end the newsmen were quick to show the ironies and the intimate scenes of war.

168. *"Fifth Avenue and Broadway meet at Twenty-Third Street in Manhattan, but in France they meet in the trenches. Our soldiers have named the paths of war after their home thoroughfares" (Committee of Public Information)*

Soldiers always seem like they are using home as a point of reference. In this photo American and French soldiers stand along a trench that US Doughboy wags have designated Broadway and Fifth Avenue.

169. *"At this point on an Italian front, a soldier, while digging with a pick-axe found his blows repelled. After striking a few blows an oddly colored particle was brought to his view which aroused his interest. A few successive blows brought to view a unique design set in the earth. While working with care he finally unearthed a perfect Roman mosaic"* (Official Italian War photo)

In the midst of destruction there were still discoveries to be made. While digging a trench an Italian soldier came across a Roman mosaic. This doesn't indicate where it was found. Note they have strung barbed wire around this find.

170. *"Alert! Gas masks for onion attack"* (Bain News Service)

Finding good use of equipment, a soldier uses a gasmask to cut onions. Humor was always a way to deal with daily life in the army.

171. *"Nails are bad for motor tires and horses' hoofs alike, so the allies have put up boxes in which to deposit those scattered about the roads, thus saving many times "nine stitches""* (Underwood & Underwood)

Whether this was practical or not, nail boxes were place along the roads to protect against flat tires which could bring all things to a grinding halt. Based on the destruction of buildings and general construction, nails could act as unintentional caltrops.

172. *"Remaining at his post to the last, Mayor Lenglet, of the city of Rheims, France, is shown preparing to leave the stricken place only when it was at the point of capture by the enemy hordes. The venerable chief official is pointing out the ruin wrought by incessant bombardment to the ancient and beautiful city. He is accompanied by Spanish officers, who were members of a neutral mission to the demolished town. In recent weeks the famous Cathedral, or what now remains of it, has been bombarded time and again for reasons known only to the Kaiser's "military strategists.""* (Underwood & Underwood)

The bravery of the allies in France extended from the military to the civilians. A Mayor in a French town about to be occupied by the Germans sees to the evacuation. The brutality of war upon the civilian population is emphasized again and again.

128 America at War

173. *"Here's the credit desk. Any man in uniform can arrange to get back to camp if his money has given out"*

Soldiers were shown being able to get credit should they run out. In the days before wire transfers or credit cards, cash was the only medium of exchange. For soldiers, supplementing their rations or equipment required cash.

174. *"If anyone imagines the life of a news correspondent in the war zone is an easy one he is very much mistaken, as in order to furnish complete and reliable information at all times these men must be in advanced and exposed positions themselves. The photo shows a number of American newspaper correspondents on a tour of inspection of the camp of occupied by U.S. Troops high in the Vosges Mountains"* (Photo International Film Services)

War correspondents had been actively covering battles since the Crimean War, but now they needed to make their way closer to the fighting and away from HQ. Notice the road is corduroyed with wood for traction. American soldiers held the line from the Moselle River to the Swiss Border. Some units were sent into the line here without much training, especially the 3rd, 4th, 36th, 78th, 91st, 79th and 89th Divisions

175. *Outpost duty for troops in the front – AWAITING THEIR COMING – One of the most difficult jobs is that of outpost duty, for you are always liable to encounter the enemy. Here is shown two British Tommies who took cover in the ruins of a house as any cover is taken in open warfare. They are ready for the Germans, who in their concentrated attack on the British army during the March offensive, forced the Tommies to fight back-to-back because the odds were so great.*

The desolation of villages after war came though created a moonscape of broken landscape. This created hiding places to observe and attack from - in this case the remnants of a house.

176. *Troops use model terrain to plan operations so they can anticipate obstacles better than just looking at maps. (British Pictorial Service)*

Airplanes and photography were able to create views of the battlefield that were used by officers in planning operation. As the war progressed allied planning recreated battlefield areas to help plan attacks and allow officers to understand their areas of responsibility.

America at War

177. *The Mess Hall of Battery E of the 312th Horse Field Artillery at Camp McClellan goes up in smoke.*

Camp McClellan is located in Anniston, Alabama. It was one of mobilization camps for inducting men into the armed forces in 1917.

178. *The sombre reality of war is that men die. Here soldiers gather to bury comrades. "The cross tells the story in three words, "Killed in Action," which appear below the line recording his name and regiment. It is the last act in the drama of a private who gave up his life for his country on the British front in France" Note the soldier is on a stretcher, covered with a blanket.*

One of the unspoken rules of media was don't show your own dead. In this case it was done to show how American soldiers honored their comrades.

World War I through the Tabloids 131

179. *To remind people of why they were fighting, here are the graves of victims from the Lusitania. "In this spot in Ireland rest the bodies of a number of victims of the Lusitania. The Cunard Line recently had sign place by the graves."*

Most likely this is Old Church Cemetery in Cobh

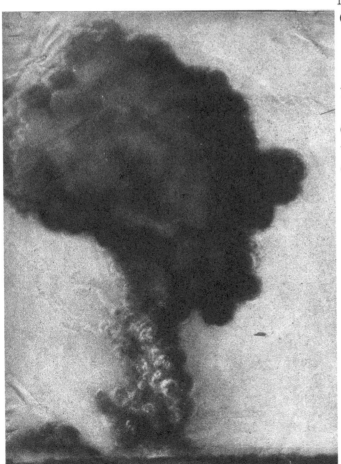

180. *The explosion at Courneuve in 1918.*

Courneuve is an area outside of Paris. There was a grenade depot there that went up in an explosion in 1918 for reasons unknown.

Gas Attacks

World War I through the Tabloids

More than 91,000 men were directly killed from poison gas and countless more were incapacitated. In January 1915, the Germans experimented with tear gas shells against the Russian before unleashing Chlorine gas at Ypres. The tear gas shells were not a success. The chlorine gas killed immediately, while the mustard gas introduced later injured the lungs and incapacitated men for the rest of their lives.

Poison gas was outlawed by the Hague Declaration of 1899 and the Hague Convention of 1907, but was used by the Germans in 1914. The first full-scale use of gas was against French, Canadian and British troops at the Second Battle of Ypres in April 1915. Consequently, it was viewed with disdain by allied audiences even though the allies used it as well.

What made gas attacks especially difficult for troops in the field is the gas always sank to the lowest level, so that it would linger in trenches and sometimes make it into dugouts. Shell holes and trenches became unlikely death-traps to unwary troops. This always required troops to keep gas masks nearby.

The French first used tear gas in grenades in 1914 with limited effect. The Germans started using Chlorine gas, with mixed results starting in 1915. Later in 1915 the French developed Phosgene gas which had much more adverse effects. In July 1917 the Germans began using Mustard Gas (sulfur mustard) with much deadlier effects. Mustard Gas that got into the soil could be active for weeks. The allies also used Mustard Gas, starting in 1917.

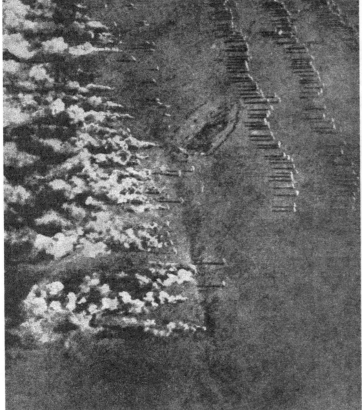

181. *Gas attack on the eastern front showing how gas was disbursed.*

In this case it looks like canisters that were opened up so that gas would move towards the opposite line. Alternatively, it could be delivered by artillery shell upon n area. The thing about gas is it is moved by wind, so if the winds started blowing a different way it could disburse the gas or blow it back toward friendly lines.

182. *The view from a trench during a gas attack. The picture on the left shows a German gas cloud approaching over "no man's land" about three seconds after the attack started. The picture on the right says, "a view of the same attack about five seconds later. This photo was actually taken in the gas cloud."*

Chlorine gas could be debilitating, but not usually deadly. With the development of Phosgene and Mustard gas, they effects were not only on the lungs, but could cause blistering on the skin. In addition to the chemical effects, it screened the accompanying troops with clouds.

183. *A sentry putting on his mask and banging the gong with his foot to alert his comrades of a gas attack.*

Communication along the trenches was still haphazard. There was telephone communication with the rear lines. But lines were often cut. Gongs and ratchets was a way to let men know about gas attacks even over the noise of shells.

184. *A wounded man having his mask put on him by a comrade. (Commission of the Gas Defense Service)*

The wounded, especially those in the lower levels of the trench were potentially the most vulnerable to gas which settled in low areas. In this picture and the previous one the trench walls were reinforced with wood fascines indicating they had been established there for some time

185. *Front line troops firing into a gas attack to stop any advancing patrols.*

Gas was used as a cover for attacking troops, used to disrupt the troops in the trenches.

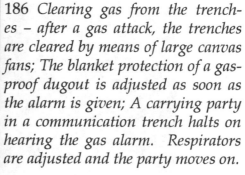

186 *Clearing gas from the trenches – after a gas attack, the trenches are cleared by means of large canvas fans; The blanket protection of a gas-proof dugout is adjusted as soon as the alarm is given; A carrying party in a communication trench halts on hearing the gas alarm. Respirators are adjusted and the party moves on.*

Dugouts descended further into the earth, so it was important to keep the gas from creeping in. Wool or flannel blankets – sometimes damped – were useful to halt gas invading the dugouts.

World War I through the Tabloids 137

187. *A work party out of the trenches waiting for the gas to clear*

As previously mentioned, troops would leave the trenches after a gas attack to let it clear before returning. There is a scene in the movie, "All Quiet on the Western Front" that details the horror gas in trenches can cause.

188. *A G.I. testing a new gas mask, showing how the gas stays low in the trench. The caption says, "Going into the gas. American soldier wearing a new gasmask, walking into the trench full of deadly fumes which are so heavy they do not rise to harm the men watching the demonstration.*

This is the equivalent of testing body armor by shooting the person wearing it. This is obviously not mustard gas as his hands are exposed.

Artillery

Since Napoleon, artillery was called "King of the Battlefield". The First World War introduced some of the largest and deadliest artillery warfare war had known up till then. Industrialization gave the world great leaps forward – the steam engine, airplanes, cars, but it also developed bigger and deadlier ways to kill people. The might of allied artillery was displayed to show how, "we can win".

189. *British Artillerymen placing a field gun in position on the Somme Front during the first days of the German Offensive (IFS)*

This takes placed during the Second Battle of the Somme (Aug – Sept 1918). This field artillery piece was the descendant of the guns that fought Napoleon. They were still moved laterally by hand at the rear. Their supply of shells is neatly piled along the side. The 18-lb gun was the standard field gun for the British during World War I.

190. *American artillerymen who fought in Picardy replacing empty 75 (mm) shells in a camouflaged ammunition carriage (French Official Photograph)*

This rotogravure picture shows the shells in a protective cover, by which they mean a canvas cover. The battery is protected by an embankment. Prior to World War I the American field gun was the 3.2-inch M1897. Upon the entry of the US into the war, the 75 mm gun based on French and British models was used by most field artillery units

191. *Battery E 112 Horse Field Artillery at Camp McClellan*

The 112th was organized in April 1917 in New Jersey and was eventually assigned to the 29th Division (Blue/Grey Division) that arrived in Brest, France in June 1918.

Camp McClellan was located in Anniston, Alabama on the site of Fort McClellan. In March 1917 the government acquired additional acreage for the construction of a National Guard training camp. It was formally established on 18 July 1917. It was one of thirty-two mobilization camps formed to train men for World War I.

The first troops arrived in late August 1917; by October there were more than 27,000 men from units in New Jersey, Virginia, Maryland, Delaware, and the District of Columbia training at the camp under the 29th Infantry Division, commanded by Major General Charles G. Morton. Other troops included the 1st Separate Negro Company of Maryland, the 6th Division, the 157th Depot Brigade, the 11th and 12th Training Battalions, and the 1st, 2nd, and 3rd Development Regiments.

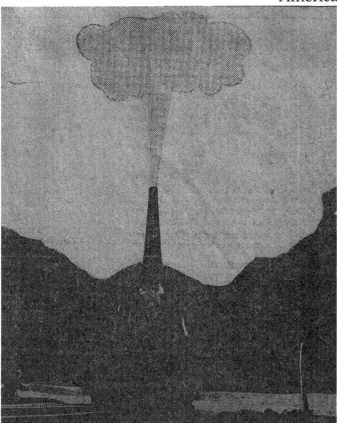

192. *This is one of the big French guns that are bombarding the long-range gun with which the Germans have been shelling Paris. This picture shows a night shot from the "Fanvette", a 340 gun. (Underwood and Underwood)*

The original photo is not clear which would go along with a "night" photo. Counter battery fire was an important part of controlling the battlefield. Guns would intimidate cities and be used on troops. Finding the location of enemy batteries would allow your guns to fire on their guns to put them out of action and give you dominance on the battlefield. As the war progressed airplanes were used to help locate enemy artillery positions. This is turn, made it important to mount artillery on movable platforms.

193. *The newest Filloux 155-Millimetre gun, named after its inventor. The troughs under the wheels allow the gun to be moved smoothly through the mud. In good going they are removed. (French Official Photograph)*

The World War I battlefields were often muddy affairs, especially after being crisscrossed by armies after four years. In some cases, they still used horses to move these heavy weapons. In this case you can see two trucks pulling the gun. Most likely, this refers to the 155 L modele 1918 Schneider

194. *"Big Lizzie" SPEAKS – A British howitzer in action. Notice the size of the shells*

This looks like a 9.2" howitzer. The shells require the attached crane to load this monster weapon. It was common and had been common to name guns.

195. *Turning, Boring and Rifling Big American guns (Committee on Public Information)*

Showing the might of US industry was a constant theme in the press once the US entered the war. Prior to the US entry it was a large supplier of steel to the world and supplied the belligerents as well. These are barrels for large field artillery and ships.

196. *Getting a howitzer into position on the front defended by the Canadian troops*

This is a BL8-inch MK VII gun with a camouflage paint scheme. In the 1880's the British navy abandoned these guns in favor of the 9 inch guns, but they were still used in the Australian navy and in the field.

World War I through the Tabloids 145

197. *Inside view of the machine shop of a plant for making artillery* (top right)

The barrel in the front left appears to be a 6-in M1903 field gun. This is an example of the industrial might of the US in the war for which the US was known as the arsenal of democracy.

198. *(Below) Armored trains are being used more and more by the French forces in stemming the desperate German thrusts toward Paris. Some of these trains are mounted with regular "battleship" guns and are moving forts of tremendous formability. The weapon shown in this photo is a 400-millimetre affair. Incidentally it – like many others – is manned by American Coast Defense gunners.*

Large guns such as this used the railroad carriage to handle the recoil and move back into position. The one handicap was it could only go where trains could go. The advantage for artillery like this is that it was mobile so counter-battery fire could be difficult to pinpoint, while track could be laid down to go in different directions. Mobile batteries like this began to see prominence by 1916.

199. *Heavily armored trains are being used by the French and have proved their worth in battle. (International Film Service/Committee on Public Information)*

The mobility of engines combined with the military advancements led to the development of armored trains. They only move along track, but they could mount heavy guns that would fire and move so that enemy artillery could not necessarily find their position. Trains usually had an infantry component and several machine guns to fend off enemy troops should they get too close. Armored trains could be rolled up to the front to bring men and equipment, but as with the large guns, were limited to the rail lines. Using interior lines for defense, however, they could be very useful to beating back attempts at a breakthrough.

200. *Artillerymen with an Italian field piece, a French invention, which is said to be superior even to the French "75" (Underwood & Underwood)*

This appears to be the cannone da 65/17 model 13 which was developed for mountain troops and infantry support. As such it had to be able to get to places, heavier artillery could not go, yet still deliver the punch needed to beat back infantry attacks.

201. *Americans moving artillery into position*

That is a horse-drawn artillery caisson in the foreground. Artillery moved by a combination of horses, trucks, tractors and trains. The closer to the front the more they relied on animal power when the terrain was churned up.

Weapons and Equipment

The weapons of war were displayed on the pages ranging from the impressive to the exotic. The might of the allied war effort was displayed to bolster confidence in the war and our troops.

Solving the riddle of poison gas was a concern of armies once it was introduced.

202. *Belgian soldiers, now fighting fiercely in Flanders, wear a combination gas mask and shrapnel helmet. The visor may be raised or lowered. (Central News Service, NY)*

A Belgian gasmask that looks like a medieval knight's helmet. The rifle is covered with a canvas protector to keep dirt out of the breech.

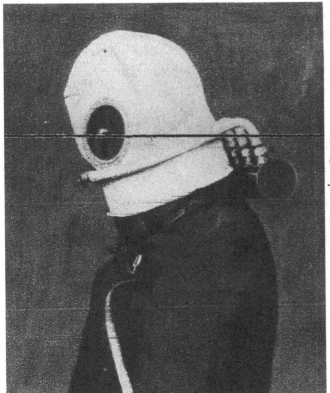

203. *As German gas is injurious to the eyes as well as the lungs, some masks are made to cover the entire face. (Kadel & Herbert)*

A hooded gas mask with a rebreather on the back. Masks such as this were hot and did not circulate air. This looks like a variation of a British "P" mask

150   America at War

204. *This type of mask; used in the city waterworks where chlorine, a deadly gas is used in the treatment of the water (Kadel & Herbert)*

Another hooded gas mask used in water treatment plants, this one with the rebreather in the front like a box mask.

205. *Although gas masks have become one of the most important items in a soldier's equipment, their use is by no means limited to warfare. The mask on the left is worn by workers in some tobacco factories as a protection against fine tobacco dust. That on the right is used by moving picture operators in scenarios containing fire and explosion scenes. (Kadel & Herbert)*

There is a popular idea that gas masks were only developed once the war started. Variations had been used among civilians prior to the war.

206. *Because chlorine is used in United States submarines, undersea crew are equipped with masks like these. (Kadel & Herbert)*

Chlorine gas in submarines was a dangerous by-product of seawater interacting with the electric batteries. This wold often require submarines to surface and vent the gas. Until they were able to do so, masks like this were needed by the crew.

World War I through the Tabloids

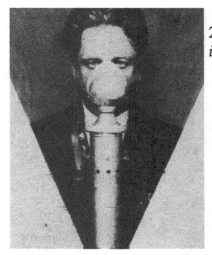

207. *This mask is for a certain kind of gas that does not affect the eyes but is very injurious to inhale. (Kadel & Herbert)*

208. *These three ghost-like figures seen in the above photographs are those of sailors aboard an Austro-Hungarian warship. They are upper deck hands and are seen her coming down from the navigation deck to take their places at the guns apparently before action. The goggled masks they wear are their protection against the noxious fumes which come from firing guns.*

These are the hooded type masks common to several countries.

209. *Protection against poison gas on the battlefront is not limited to men but is extended to horses beyond the lines. This picture shows how the mask is fitted over the horse's muzzle. (International Film Service)*

Thousands of horses were lost through combat. In some cases, box respirators were used for horses like men, covering the whole head. All armies used devices like this for men and horses by the end of the war.

210. *A corner in a great shop where projectiles of many sizes are bored and turned to size. (Passed by the Committee on Public Information)*

This photo again shows the might of allied production – although it does not tell where it is. The 1915 "crisis" on a shortage of shells led to the fall of Asquith's government and the rise of Lloyd George. One line of strategy held that artillery could win the war.

211. *Capping 14-inch shells.*

These were shells for the big guns – battleships and heavy artillery. Until they were capped off the shells were not as dangerous.

World War I through the Tabloids   153

212. *A Bogie load of shells*

In this case "Bogie" means "Truckload". These shells do not have the fuse attached yet.

213. *British machine gun men getting the range on a position from which a German raid is expected. There are probably a row of these guns waiting for Fritz. (Photo by Central News)*

This looks to be a Vickers Medium gun, which weighed between 33 and 51 lbs, shot a .303 shell with an effective range of 2,200 yards. As it stated in the photo, these were set up in groups of interlocking fire to cut down troops crossing no-man's land. Artillery was used to try to take out these guns and in turn created shell holes that were used as cover.

154   America at War

214. *A French 75mm anti-aircraft gun ready for action. The gunners are waiting for a Boche flyer, that has been sighted, to come within range. (International Film Service)*

This was known as the "Canon de 75 antiaérien mle. 1913-1917" It was manufactured by Schneider firing a 6.25 kg shell up to 6.5 km. In this case the gun is situated in a depression.

215. *French General with an unexploded German bomb*

The name of the general is not indicated, but the aerial bomb appears to be a 661 lb. device. Duds or unexploded bombs and shells are still being uncovered. In France more than 900 tons and in Belgium 200 tons of unexploded ordinance are uncovered each year.

216. *Captured Helmets Exhibited Here. Another exhibit of German war relics is being held in this country. This time the Belgians. The Italians recently held an exhibition at Madison Square Garden. The Belgian officials have opened an exhibit at The American Art Galleries showing some of the relics captured by Belgian soldiers fighting in Flanders. The above photo shows two types of helmets, at the right is the German military parade helmet, while on the left is the German steel trench helmet. (Kadel and Herbert, NY)*

As in the American Civil War there were in war exhibitions of captured enemy equipment that included uniforms, weapons and photographs as a way to bolster support for the allies. The pickelhaube on the right was made of leather, later felt and worn with a canvas cover early in the war. By 1916, the pickelhaube was replaced the steel helmet (stahlhelm) on the left. The plate on the pickelhaube would indicate that this comes from Prussia. Exhibitions like this also was a way to get contributions from the public to support the war effort.

217. *One of the reinforced concrete machine gun "pill boxes" in which American machine gunners and outpost detachments receive instruction in their training camps in France (Committee on Public Information by I.F.S.)*

The term "pill box" dates to 1916 – 1917 which referred to a type of blockhouse or a concrete dug-in with firing loopholes. This particular pill box has a concrete approach passageway. The ports in the front held machine guns or light calibre guns. It is reinforced concrete which is impervious to all but direct hits from artillery.

218. *Fountains of Death – Two big German shells bursting before the British lines at Picardy.*

Real photos of artillery across a broken landscape

219. *American soldiers putting an anti-aircraft machine gun in position in a village on the Flanders front which German fliers are continually attacking. (French Official Photograph)*

They are holding a Hotchkiss M1914 machine gun which weighed 50 lbs, fired an 8mm shell from a strip of 24 to 30 rounds and a range of 2,400 yards. The Americans purchased 7,000 guns in 1917 to 1918.

220. *Captured Trophies From the Picardy Front. It would take many good sized museums to hold and display all the interesting German trophies captured by the British and French in the battle of Picardy last month. The booty ranges from the most worthless trinkets taken from prisoners to the latest type of big guns. Here is a roomful of the booty. Incidentally the photograph is one of a series of the first of the battle to reach this country. (Underwood & Underwood)*

These are French officers. In the forefront are maxim machine guns. The weapon in the hands of the officer on the right is a German Assault Rifle, the Bergmann MP18-1 which was introduced in 1918.

Vehicles and Infernal Machines

The First World War ushered in the mechanized age of warfare and with that came photos of machines many had never seen. Although trucks and tractors were common place by 1917, a good portion of men, material and equipment were still moved along by horses. The U.S. Army was becoming mechanized; and that technology was applied to all sorts of vehicles by both sides.

Even with mechanization, guns were generally moved close to the front lines by train and from there moved by horse and/or tractor to a firing position.

221. *One of Many Thousands. In the details of war this photo shows an American "donkey" engine in the act of lowering to a French wharf one of the motor trucks that are essential to the United States Army supply, and which are being sent over by the thousands. These trucks are being used in every sector of the army. (Committee of Public Information)*

The use of a mechanical "donkey engine" crane moving a flatbed truck from a ship to the wharf for use by U.S. troops. This truck was Class-B Standardized Military or "Liberty" truck. It was designed by the Quartermaster Corps with standardized parts. It was manufactured by over fifteen automotive manufacturers that delivered over ten thousand trucks to France.

World War I through the Tabloids

222. *An American armored engine amidst the ruins of a French village.*

To protect trains from attacks, since the American Civil War, armies increasingly made use of armored trains. Here is an example of an armoured engine towing some transport cars. Sometimes this was simply moving men and material who were subject to artillery fire and planes. It came to include trains that were essentially mobile artillery.

223. *One of our new army tractors blithely climbs a tree, hauling a 4.7-inch gun along. (Underwood & Underwood)*

This is a Holt tractor showing its dexterity. Because the modern battlefield of 1918 was a churned up and muddy place movement of equipment via horses was difficult. Tractor's allowed men and material to move around the battlefield. These mechanical developments accelerated the design of tanks that relied on the metal treads to navigate difficult terrain.

224. *Camouflaged French armored cars lined up along the road in the once beautiful Somme country where hundreds of thousands of friend and foe have perished in the great battles that have been fought in that section. (Photo International Film Service)*

French Peugeot Armoured cars camouflaged in the countryside with foliage By this point in the war vehicles were often painted in camouflage patterns. These cars were used for scouting along roads.

224. *A train of flat cars loaded with howitzers starting on their long journey to the battle front in France. (Committee on Public Information)*

12-inch Howitzers being moved by flatbed trains to the front. These guns were shipped by boat, offloaded to trains, moved to the front via horses, then tractors. This was part of the mechanized cycle of warfare.

225. *An A7V knocked on its side.*

Despite their innovations in inter-war tank design, German designed tanks "A7V" were big, boxy contraptions. Here is one such vehicle 542 which has number "35" on the from named "Elfriede" which was abandoned at Villers-Bretonneux on 28 April 1918, recovered by the British in May, and handed over to the French. It was displayed in the Palace de la Concorde in Paris in 1918. Notice the tow-rope cabling on the top along with camouflage. This is the rear of the vehicle. Compare this to the next view and it appears the name was written on the front and back.

226. *German Tank Put Out of Action by British Shell Fire. Here is a photograph of one of the captured German tanks copied from the British tank but built so top-heavy that they were unable to negotiate crater holes, stone walls or corduroy roads like the less unwieldy British caterpillars. Means of egress are shown by the openings in the bottom of the tank, used as emergency exits to clear the turning gear of the mud when the fighting machine is stuck, or to escape without being observed. The British and French tanks are now of two kinds, known as "male" and "female", the "male" being the larger of the two and capable of ploughing through the most formidable obstacles, while the "female" is used in advance of light infantry and on less obstructed ground. This tank upturned shows in its peak the revolving turret with its four-inch gun. It was put out of action by shell fire on the fighting around Montdidier around the Aisne front.*

This is another view of the same tank; however, it is from the front. The front gun was in the chassis with a 45-degree firing arc. This picture shows a great view of the underchasse design.

World War I through the Tabloids 165

227. *A British tank hit by German shells are inspected by French troops shows the devastation a shell can do to an armored vehicle.*

On the front part of the tank to the right is the date 9 October 1918.

228. *United in peace as well as in war: French soldier using an American tractor for his spring ploughing. This photograph was taken within sound of the Picardy battle. (Kadel & Herbert)*

The ideal of the normalcy of ploughing fields might have seemed at home to American's where there was still a large rural population. At a time when France still needed to feed its population, using soldiers and military equipment might not have been that far-fetched.

The Air War

The first acknowledged heavier than air flight was recognized as the Wright Brothers in 1903. It wasn't until 1905 that airplane flights were sustainable for significant periods. By the outbreak of the war, airplanes had still only been used for racing and limited military applications. They were not armed to fire forward until 1915, and were not initially efficient bombers.

During this period, the U.S. Army and Navy had their own flight branches. For the most part on the Western Front this was called the, "U.S. Air Service", they were a branch of the Army similar to infantry or cavalry.

Aeronautic technology developed rapidly during the war in Europe for their military applications. Zeppelins – large gas filled balloons that were powered by engines and capable of traversing long distances to bomb places like London. In the United States, airplane technology lagged behind technology and designs that the war in Europe were developing – the U.S. Army punitive expedition against Poncho Villa in 1916 still used open-framed, rear engine Wright flyers (also known as "pushers") and Curtiss "Jenny" two-seaters, while more sophisticated planes were in Europe.

By 1918 airplanes had developed specialized roles – there were scouts, fighters and bombers. Although the U.S. had developed very powerful engines to use in airplanes, most of the planes used by American flyers were of European manufacture and design. The home front wanted to know that U.S. flyers were capable of meeting "the Huns" in the air and defeat them.

At the same time, because of aerial reconnaissance people started to see views of cities and land that they had never seen before. The air service supported all the branches of service - helping in artillery spotting and counter-battery fire, infantry support and blimps.

229. *Made in the USA. While the nation is stirred by the charges of alleged graft in the carrying out of the aeroplane program filed by Gutzon Borglum, it is interesting to note that the much-criticized Liberty motor has been a great success in training planes. The training plane is vastly different from the battle plane, but it is quite as important, as the aviators must learn to fly with it before they are prepared to handle the greater air craft.*

Gutzon Borglum was a sculptor of some note who worked on buildings and other projects such Stone Mountain and Mount Rushmore. He was a member of the Klu Klux Klan. Borglum investigated "malpractice" in US aircraft manufacturing that he delivered to President Wilson. President Wilson tried to distance himself from Borglum from this early conspiracy theorist.   (https://forgottennewsmakers.com/2010/08/03/gutzon-borglum-1867-1941-sculptor-of-mount-rushmore/)

This is an American Jenny 2-seated flyer. Although the Jenny was in production since 1915 it was considered too underpowered to fly in combat. It was still considered a valuable trainer and most pilots in the U.S. and Canadian air corps learned to fly using them prior to combat.

230. *The Start of the Loop-the-loop. An American plane preparing to "zoom" with her nose straight up in the air and her guiding planes at the perpendicular preparatory to make a glorified switchback which is an ordinary stunt with an "Ace". (US Marine Publicity)*

An American Jenny in flight overhead. Even though these planes never saw combat in Europe, they were touted in the American press – in part due to the controversy on American planes being behind Europe.

231. *An American Ace. Allan F. Winslow one of the premier American aviators now in France about to start on an observation tour and probably take a chance on being "Archied" as his stalls over the German front. (Committee on Public Information)*

Lt. Allan F. Winslow is also listed as "Alan". As part of the 94th "Hat in the Ring" squadron, he shot down the first German plane by a U.S. pilot along with Lt. Douglas Campbell on 14 April 1918 in a Nieuport N.28. He shot down a second plane on 6 June 1918 and was subsequently wounded in combat on 31 July 1918, losing an arm in the process. He was captured and spent the remainder of the war as a POW. With only two "kills" he was not a true ACE which required a minimum of five confirmed kills, but he as an early hero. "Archied" was a slang term for getting into trouble.

232. *Loading up for a Raid. The care British aviation mechanics give the planes trusted in their care. Here they are seen adjusting aerial bombs to the fall line of a plane that is about to start on a bombing trip. The slightest error in adjusting the bomb to the trigger line means failure on the part of the observer to drop the destructive missile, which is winged and flanged like a torpedo and whistles earthward at an inconceivable velocity. (British Official Photo)*

Despite efforts to increase the accuracy of bombing through World War II, precision bombing was a hit or miss affair.

233. *Embryo Aviators and Their Instructors. The plane here is part of the intricate system of aviation instruction. It is called a "Grass Cutter" the wings being clipped so that it cannot rise above six feet above the ground it is used in teaching control to young aviator at an aviation school in France. (Committee on Public Information)*

Access to powerful machines required intensive training before being sent into the air. No one mastered this process until they survived long enough or were killed. It was a new technology that was used to the maximum advantage.

America at War

234. (previous page, bottom) Another view of the same photo

235. *This isn't a bad negative of an American hydroplane. The vibration was made by a machine gun shooting between the revolutions of the propeller as the picture was taken during a test in a French port. (Kadel & Herbert)*

      This is a U.S. navy hydroplane (seaplane). While they often used the N9 a version of the Jenny, this seems to be a Thomas-Morse S4C. Keep in mind the ability to shoot a machine gun through a propeller using interrupter gear had only come into existence in 1915 and was still amazing to most folks back home.

236. *Sixteen American planes fly in battle formation. This official photograph was taken at Rockwell Field, San Diego, CA (Committee of Public Information)*

Rockwell Field was an Army-Air base on the Coronado Peninsula that was also the home of the Curtiss School of Aviation which was founded in 1912. The Army Signal Corps Aviation Group was founded there in 1917. Both Army and Navy pilots trained in Curtiss and Wright planes. Rockwell Field was named after 2nd Lt. Lewis Rockwell who was killed in a crash of a Wright Model B in 1912. Little things like maintaining flight formation was important as planes went into combat.

237. *A plane returning at sunset from photo reconnaissance.*

Two seat bombers were used for aerial reconnaissance that was needed by both the infantry and artillery. This one looks to be a DeHavilland DH4, many of which were built in the U.S.

238. *Take off for the first American daylight bombing raid into Germany.*

This is the 96th Squadron which flew Breguet 14's. Over 600 Breguet's were used by the US Army during the war. This was the 96th "Devil's Head" squadron in formation. The 96th served as part of the 1st Day Bombardment Group supporting the French Eight and First US Army from June to November 1918.

239. *An American "Big-Game Hunter in France, and his Morning's "Bag".*

An unidentified American flyer with an Albatros D.III forced down behind allied lines

240. *This is America's first real air trophy. It was brought down near Nancy. Americans have destroyed Hun planes before, but not flying under their own colors.*

Before the US entered the war, American citizens joined the armed forces of other countries. Seventeen Americans earned the title of "ACE" in the French air force and fifty-three in the British air corps. The first victories credited to American-trained pilots came on April 14, 1918, when Lieutenants Alan F. Winslow and Douglas Campbell of the 94th Pursuit Squadron – this photo could be referring to them.

241. *Captured Gotha's brought down by Americans.*

Although the magazine has called this plane a "Gotha", it looks like a Pfalz DIII.

242. *Night flight at Le Bourget.*

Le Bourget was a military airport outside of Paris and today hosts an airport museum. The aircraft looks like a Voisin 8 French scout/bomber used by French and American pilots.

243. *Reconnaissance on the French front.*

A scout flying low above a destroyed French Village. This looks like a British or American plane – possibly a Bristol F2

244. *Operations of enemy aircraft over the Eastern seaboard will be made exceedingly difficult by this latest type of searchlights. The apparatus shown here is part of the Mobile Anti-Aircraft Section of the Engineering Corps, at the Washington Barracks, Washington, DC. There are many searchlights like this doing service in France. (Committee of Public Information)*

Enemy planes never made it to the US. Searchlights were used to find enemy aircraft at night or when bounced off clouds, could create "artificial moonlight" to illuminate the battlefield. A searchlight like this was made by the Edison company.

245. *A Sausage balloon and its crew*

This was also known as a "barrage balloon". Barrage balloons were used to create barriers to low flying enemy planes. These balloons were often attached to a series of steel cables, sometimes joined to other balloons with netting. They could be raised to the level bombers would fly, and by the end of the war they covered 50 miles around London. In the foreground is an armored car and a touring car (for the officer no doubt!).

246. *Watchful Eyes That Never Close. Giant British dirigibles, like the one shown here, are playing a big and ever bigger part in guarding the coasts of the "tight little Isles" from submarine and zeppelin attacks. The big airships are on duty day and night, and, due to the elevations they attain, command a range of vision miles in excess of that of water craft. The dirigible shown in the photo is one of the newest of England's growing aerial fleet. It was snapped just as it was taking to the air. (British Official Photo)*

A British Dirigible on the watch. Dirigible is the shortened name for "Dirigible Balloon", meaning "steerable balloon". Dirigibles were used for scouting for enemy ships and subs, bombing and reconnaissance.

247. *Observation balloon used by American army officers on the French front and handled by American soldiers. Our balloon section is in its infancy yet, but is growing so rapidly it will soon pass the older European organizations. (Underwood & Underwood)*

An American observation balloon of the Caquot design. Observation balloons were fixed in place to be used by artillery spotting the effectiveness of shots. Because of their importance, some pilots specifically targeted destroying them and earned the title of, "Balloon Busters". This was hazardous duty because of the anti-aircraft defenses that often surrounded them. American Ace, Lt. Frank Luke, was well-known for taking on balloons.

248. *One of Britain's bombing squadrons ready for a daylight raid over the German lines. Terror is growing fast in the areas visited as immense damage results. (Underwood & Underwood)*

A squadron of British bombers used in daylight bombing runs. These look like Bristol F.2's or DH-4's which were workhorse bombers for the British and later American air forces.

249. *A group of Allied aviation officers inspecting the latest Caproni triplane. In the centre are the Caproni brothers, the inventors and next an American officer.*

These are Caproni Triplane Bombers. This looks like a Ca42/52 with the nose marking of a British Squadron. Caproni's were used by the Italian, British and the U.S. air services. Giovanni "Gianni" Caproni is in the center. He was born is in Austrian territory and opened his airplane manufacturing company in 1911. He focused his war years on bombers.

250. *Exclusive view of four of the powerful new Caproni triplanes ready for flight on the Italian front. (Photos Press Ill Co.)*

Another view of Caproni bombers, a version of the Ca.4. Notice the ladder used to climb into the plane.

World War I through the Tabloids 181

251. *A German high-altitude aviator putting on his electrically heated gloves.*

This is a German High-Altitude flyer with electrical gloves and a warm jacket. It should be kept in mind that these were open cockpit planes with no heat, so pilots needed to stay warm to maneuver planes properly and avoid frostbite. More than likely this man was part of a bomber crew.

252. This was a composite photo of a German Albatross dropping a bomb. The magazine combined the two photos for effect and get the reading public interested in it.

253. *A zeppelin brought down by the Royal Flying Corps*

The remains of a zeppelin shot down by the British. Zeppelin's were framed by steel, covered with fabric and powered by motors. They often had some armament and were used for long-range bombing. Because they were flown at high altitudes, they were often not seen until they were upon a target, hence the Allied press played up their "unsportsmanlike" aspect. The air service allowed military planners and the civilian readers views of the war and the countryside they had not seen before.

254. *A broken road, taken from a kite balloon. In the center of the picture may be seen a windless used in hauling down the balloon.*

A "kite balloon" – the equivalent of today's hot air balloon is above a corduroy road. This consisted of logs cut in half and laid in the ground for easy passage over the muddy fields in Flanders. The shadows are people on the ground as well as the truck.

255. *The photograph above taken from an aeroplane gives one of the most excellent idea of what a gas attack is really like. The deadly gas fumes are being set free from the French trenches and the wind blowing towards the German lines carries them into the enemy trenches. The Germans were first to introduce poison gas as an implement of warfare.*

Photos like this were new and showed the terror of gas on the front lines. In this case gas is released from canisters.

256. *An interesting aerial view of the Citadel of Dwinsk.*

This is a view of the citadel of Dwinsk in Russia (now Daugavpils, Latvia) a major fortress and rail center in Russia.

257. *Photograph of Cambria [sic], made by a German aviator who flew over the historic battle ground during the heat of battle and later captured by a British airman. His photographic apparatus was found uninjured and this picture was registered by his camera as having been made from an altitude of 2,000 ft. (International Film Service)*

Cambrai, the site of a battle from 20 November to 7 December in 1917 and 8-10 October 1918.

World War I through the Tabloids 187

258. *The city of Verona, Italy as it looks from an aeroplane. It is one of the most beautiful cities that country [sic] of wonderful art and architecture. The huge Amphitheatre dating back to the days of the Romans can be seen in the center. The city contains many famous picture galleries and a magnificent old cathedral that is well known to travelers. (Underwood & Underwood)*

On the Water

If the U.S. Army was not prepared for a foreign war, the U.S. Navy was ready to go into action. Being a mercantile nation, the navy was an important part of U.S. foreign policy. United States destroyers took part in convoy system that escorted merchant ships across the Atlantic.

The military fleet was not only on display in the papers, but the merchant fleet as well. Merchant seaman risked their lives as part of the convoys and local shipping. At the same time, shipyards up and down the east coast began a renaissance of boat building in the U.S. turning out ships in steel, wood and concrete.

The merchant fleet, however, had fallen behind the development of other nations, and the loss of ships from submarines required a concerted effort in order to keep supplies flowing to Europe. To help in the need for merchant shipping, the Emergency Fleet Corp was established on 16 April 1917 to acquire, maintain, and operate merchant ships to meet national defence, foreign and domestic commerce during World War I. It was renamed the U.S. Shipping Board Merchant Fleet Corporation in 1927 and abolished by Congress in 1936 under the merchant marine act. The government commandeered available shipyards and were able to produce ships within 94 days. By the end of the war, four major shipyards were producing more annual tonnage than any country.

Because of the influx of recruits, Naval Training Centers sprang up on the east and west coast. Some of these were closed after the war only to be revived in the 1940's, while others were developed further.

The power and sacrifices of other nations were also showcased, especially the up-and-coming superpower in the east – Japan

259. *The turret of a battleship under construction. "Erecting a 14-inch gun turret"*

The 14" (356 mm) gun was introduced to the U.S. Navy in 1914 for the USS Texas and New York. They initially fired a 1,400 lb (640 kg) armor-piercing (AP) projectiles. The guns could fire a shell 23,000 yd (21,000 m). Each individual gun weighed 142,492 lb (64,633 kg) with the breech and measured 53 ft 6.5 in (16.32 m) in length.

260. *The call for the allies was for the U.S. to build more ships to make sure they replace losses from German submarines. This is a rudder for a ship being built in Philadelphia.*

Although there was a naval yard in Philadelphia from 1775, the main naval yard dated from 1870 to 1995. In 1917 the Naval Aircraft factory was established there.

261. *Shipbuilding in Texas. Rapid wartime construction of anything was part of the marvel of modern industrialization. Note that wooden frames are being used to shape the hulls. "Many Gulf coast cities that never before engages in shipbuilding are now engaged in a thriving business. This photo shows two huge vessels on the way at a Texas yard where ships are being turned out with astonishing rapidity." (Underwood and Underwood)*

The Emergency Fleet Corp (EFC) was established by the United States Shipping Board on 16 April 1917 to acquire, maintain and operate merchant ships. The Shipping Board was established when the US was at peace, but the EFC was established for a war economy. Congress rejected attempts by President Wilson to establish a shipping board until 1916.

The EFC was a corporation with one shareholder – the US Government – whose authority was to acquire or construct shipping. An initial program looked to construct a fleet of small wooden steamers, but they resulted in a large number of ships with no practical purpose in a modern war.

This pushed manufacturers to mass produce steel and even a concrete ship for the fleet.

262. *"The first steel ship built south of Newport News is shown here just after launching. It is the USS Mesoil, a vessel of 3,000 tons built by the Alabama-New Orleans Transportation Company. The launching of this vessel proves the possibility of shipbuilding at New Orleans." (Underwood and Underwood)*

See the above note – shipbuilding went from wood to steel. The war spurred investment in modernizing industry across the country, shipbuilding was included. The Alabama-New Orleans Transportation Company moved coal up and down the Mississippi River.

263. *Charles M. Schwab turned Bethlehem Steel into one of the largest manufacturing operations in the world – The gentleman in the center of the group is Mr. Charles M. Schwab, who has lately been appointed director-general of the Emergency Fleet Corporation. Mayor Smith of Philadelphia is seen at the left, and Mr. Joseph Widener on the right. (International Film Service)*

Charles Schwab replaced Charles Piez at the EFC in April 1918. He instituted fixed price contracts for the construction of ships. Mr. Widener was a racehorse and art enthusiast who helped to develop modern horse racing and benefactor to the National Art Gallery in Washington, D.C.

264. *The almost obsolete industry of wooden shipbuilding has been revived as if by magic and yards for the construction of big wooden vessels like this have been springing up all along the Atlantic coast. (International Film Service)*

A revival of wooden ship building was cheap and with available material, but it was controversial in that after the war, shippers wanted steel ships. The maritime fleet had a great deal of wooden ships that no one wanted. Other materials such as concrete were also employed. The last one of these being the USS *Atlantus* off Cape May, NJ.

265. *"Two of our many new destroyers laid down since the war began on the ways at an Eastern port and almost ready for launching. Note the names of the famous naval heroes, Gamble and Breese." (Committee on Public Information)*

The destroyers Breese and Gamble under construction. These were Wickes Class destroyers launched in May 1918 and later converted to minelayers in World War II. The Breese was commissioned in October 1918. They were built at Newport News. The names are barely visible on the bow of the ships.

266. *The U.S. Naval Training Station in Bilboa Park, California use sailors to spell out the word, "Navy". "Only men to have had experience in drilling will realize how difficult it was to line up thousands of sailors in the formation shown here". (The World, 21 April 1918)*

The Navy leased land and buildings for a Naval Training Station at Bilboa Park in 1917. This was the first step in an effort to establish a permanent NTS in San Diego. This was finally realized in 1921.

267. *Another merchant ship is launched*

Once it finally got going the EFC was able to push shipbuilding production. Hog Island in Philadelphia was able to launch a ship every 5.5 days in 1918.

World War I through the Tabloids

268. *"One of the survivors of the S.S. Carolina with his coat torn by shrapnel from a U-boat off the Jersey Coast" (Underwood and Underwood)*

The SS *Carolina* was one of six ships sunk in a single day by German Submarine U-151 on 2 June 1918 off of Atlantic City. Reminiscent of Operation Drumbeat in World War II, the U.S. east coast did not adhere to strict blackouts and the mid-Atlantic coast was a hunting ground for U-boats. Most of this was blocked out of the news reporting.

269. *The USS President Lincoln on the lookout for U-boats.*

After five voyages from New York to France, carrying over 23,000 troops, she was attacked and sunk by U-90 on 31 May 1918.

270. *Sailor on guard duty at Newport Training School.*

The Naval Training Station at Newport Rhode Island was first established in the 1870. With the advent of World War I the facility was not equipped to deal with the influx of sailors requiring the construction of temporary tent barracks, then tar paper wooden building. They serviced over 5,000 men per day and helped send over 65,000 men overseas.

271. *Boat drill off Cape May's naval reserve station*

In 1917 the navy took over an old amusement park at Sewell Point as a training and section base. Aspects of the amusement park rides were incorporated into the base. When the Park burn in 1918 a proper barracks was built in its place.

World War I through the Tabloids 197

272. *Sailors carrying coal at Rodman's Neck in the Bronx.*

During World War I the US Army and Navy had training facilities at Rodman's Neck in what was a park. The 105th and 108th Infantry regiments trained there before shipping overseas. It returned to a park after the war and was once again a naval Training Station in World War II

273. *American Depot Ship at sea.*

Depot Ships are also called "Tenders" used to repair or maintain ships at sea. Before World War II, naval ships relied on tenders to move men and material between the shore and sea, as well as moving supplied for a group of ships.

274. *The American Fleet at sea in the Atlantic*

    There were no grand fleet battles involving the American navy in World War I. From the outset, the navy escorted troop ships and supplies across the Atlantic. By far U-boats were the greatest threat to shipping and the navy between 1917 and 1918.
    Because of a petroleum fuel shortage only coal burning ships were sent across the Atlantic. Division Nine contained five dreadnought era battleships - initially The *New York*, *Delaware*, *Florida* and *Wyoming*. The *Texas* was added later.

World War I through the Tabloids 199

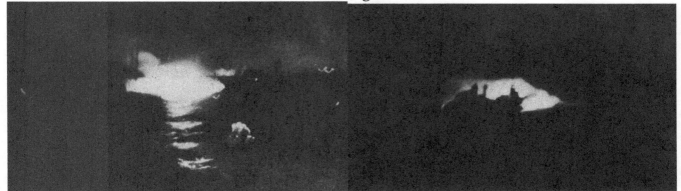

275. *Only photographs taken of the American Navy's Most Heroic Achievement. These night pictures record the rescue of thirty-four of the crew of the crew of the munition ship Florence H, following the explosion which destroyed her in French waters on April 17 last. Sixty officers and men of the American navy have been recommended for their valor that night. Amid two hundred huge powder boxes exploding constantly to the leeward of the wreck, Lieut. Haislip, at the risk of detonating his own depth-charges, dashed in with his ship, picking up survivors in the blistering heat. Quartermaster Upton and Ship's Cook Covington leaped boldly into the water to save the men clinging to the powder boxes. The large white spot is the flame of the burning ship outlined against it is Haislip's warship and close by but unable to approach because of its wooden decks is a large converted yacht. The small white spots are powder boxes exploding.*

The munitions ship *SS Florence* H exploded in Quiberon Bay off Brittany on 17 April 1918. It is generally viewed that she was torpedoed. Survivors were picked up by the *USS Truxton* and later transferred to the transport ship *USS America*.

276. *A navy dirigible above the conning tower of a battleship on the lookout for U-boats.*

The Japanese attack on the Russian Fleet at Port Arthur in the Russo-Japanese War (1904-5) showed the vulnerability of battleships to torpedoes. At this point scout planes on battleships were in their infancy, therefore dirigibles were the best way to get height to potentially see submarines. Keep in mind that during World War I submarines often cruised above the water until they found potential targets when they descended and only a periscope was visible.

277. *Airing out bedding on a battleship*

After weeks at sea with little airflow and unwashed bodies, this was the best way to keep them "fresh"

278. *Cleaning out the barrel of a 14th inch gun*

These were the big guns of the navy. Each gun fired a 1,400 lb (640 kg) shell that required four 105 lb. (48 kg) silk bags of powder, so there was a lot to clean.

World War I through the Tabloids   201

279. *Crew of the USS Oklahoma sending up an anti-aircraft target*

The Oklahoma was commissioned in 1914 but could not join Division Nine because of fuel restrictions. In 1917 she was retrofit with two 3in guns in front of the mainmast for antiaircraft defence. In August 1918 it was sent across the Atlantic with Battle Division Six and paired with the Nevada. In 1941 both ships were in the Pacific Squadron when the Japanese attacked them at Pearl Harbor.

280. *On the Trail of the "Subs". Three of Uncle Sam's boys, modern powder monkeys, are seen here carrying charges of cordite shell explosive to the five-inch gun turret. This charge is sufficient to blow any U-boat to pieces. The vigilance our navy, employing the latest methods of marine warfare, is making the activities of the enemies undersea pirates more and more difficult on this side of the Atlantic as well as Europe. (International)*

Many submarines attacked on the surface with torpedoes in order to get a clear shot.

281. *Torpedo entering the water.*

A torpedo launched from a battleship. Many ships, above the water were equipped to launch torpedoes should they get within range. Torpedoes were limited to visual targets and were not as accurate as those during the second world war.

282. *The USS Arizona sailing in New York Harbor.*

The USS *Arizona* was the last of the Pennsylvania class "Super Dreadnoughts", launched in 1916. It was never sent to Europe and was also sunk at Pearl Harbor.

World War I through the Tabloids 203

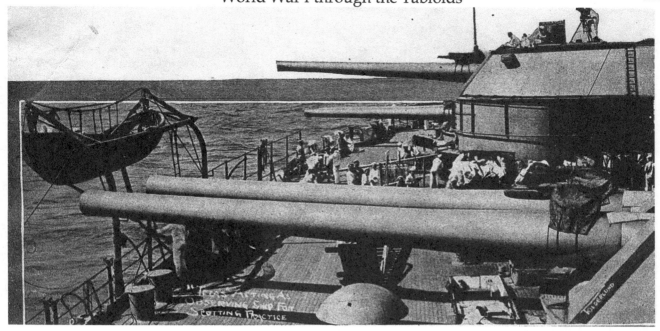

283. *The battleship USS Texas spotting for target practice*

The USS *Texas* was a New York class battleship. She was commissioned in 1914 and was sent to Europe with Division Nine. She survived both world wars and is retired in Houston. She is the only remaining pre-World War I era steel battleship.

284. *Throwing a smokescreen at sea*

As in a land battle, throwing a smoke screen obscured the view of ships on the water. This also meant that submarines could not get a clear target as well.

285. *Sailors in a bunker 70 feet underground in a French port*

Air bombardment forced people underground. Not for the claustrophobic.

286. *British sea scouts off the coast at Cornwall, England signaling*

Even though there were wireless' available, signaling by flags was still a method of communication.

World War I through the Tabloids

287. *British and Jap Sea fighters on guard. Japanese and British war vessels are shown here at the port at Vladivostok. The Japanese battleship in the distance has just landed troops to aid in the preservation of order and protection of stores and munitions for the Russian Government supplied before the collapse of the Kerensky regime by the United States. (Photo by Underwood & Underwood)*

With the collapse of the Kerensky Government the allies tired to safeguard arms and munitions they had provided the Russians to avoid them falling into the hands of the Soviets. Interventions in Vladivostok and Murmansk led to live fire between the two belligerents.

288. *Launching the new Japanese cruiser Tenryu at the Yokosuka Naval Yard. The vessel is notable in that it is made entirely of Japanese steel. (Western Newspaper Union)*

Japanese Cruiser *Tenryu* launched at their naval yard in March 1918. She was based on British designs to be used as the flagship of destroyer flotillas. She was sunk in 1943.

289. *This motorboat has an important war job. It lies in a French port waiting to go to the rescue of American hydroplanes if they get into trouble scouting.*

Hydroplanes were also known as flying boats – they could take off and land on the water. The Allies used them to scout submarine activity off the coast.

290. *A ship in convoy exploding at night*

A convoy attacked by German submarines

World War I through the Tabloids

291. *Glorious close of the HMS* Vindictive's *career, when concrete laden, she blocked the Hun U-boat base at Ostend. Commander A.C. Godsal was killed when swinging the old cruiser across the harbor channel, but a small boat took off most survivors.*

The HMS *Vindictive*, an 1890's cruiser used as a blockade ship. Early in 1918 she was fitted out for the Zeebrugge Raid. Most of her guns were replaced by howitzers, flame-throwers and mortars. On 23 April 1918 she was in fierce action at Zeebrugge when she went alongside the Mole, and her upper works were badly damaged by gunfire.

People of Note

World War I through the Tabloids

The public is always fascinated by the activities of the rich and famous, especially when it comes to war. The U.S. Public knew the major players from their photos in the papers and magazines. How they were viewed could be slanted by the type of photo as well, how it was posed and how the captioned read.

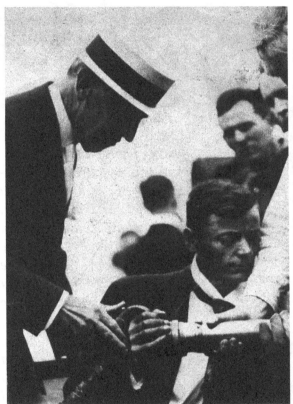

292 – *President Wilson examining war artifacts*

Woodrow Wilson (1856 – 1924) was in his second term as President of the United States in 1918, having campaigned in 1916 under the slogan, "He kept us out of War" in regard to the European conflict. By January 1918 he had issued his famous "Fourteen Points" for the basis of peace. He was not very communicative with politicians with his grand vision for America or the Peace. He did not appear as often in print as did his surrogates such as Newton Baker.

293 – *Crown Prince Frederick Wilhelm of Germany who – sooner or later – must pay the penalty for the millions of lives they have sacrificed to perpetuate the Hohenzollern's ambitions.*
Crown Prince Frederick Wilhelm (1882 – 1951) Was an active Army commander during the World War I eventually being given command of the Crown Prince's Corps. He took part of the fighting at Verdun and in the Spring Offensive. After the war he went into exile in the Netherlands before returning to Germany as a citizen in the 1920's.

294 – *Edward Albert – Prince of Wales, and heir to the English throne, is taking a very active part in the war, and according to all reports is giving a good account of himself.*

Edward Albert would become Edward VIII (1894 – 1972). He was a dashing officer, but a bit of a rake, eventually abdicating his throne for American divorcee Wallis Simpson.
He actually received support from the British public for his active participation at the front.

295 – *Here is a very interesting photograph of a meeting between Premier Clemenceau, of France, and Field Marshal Sir Douglas Haig, the gallant commander of the British forces holding the front between Vimy Ridge and the sea. M. Clemenceau spent several years in the United States as an exile, occupying the same house as Louis Napoleon did in Twelfth Street. The French Premier married a Stamford (Conn.) school teacher. In the New York Public Library there is an interesting memento of the French Premier's exile in America – a copy of his own book in which he inscribed his name and a dedicatory preface. (Official British Photo)*

George Clemenceau (1841 – 1929) was exiled protesting against Napoleon III, lived in New York City from 1865-1869 and married an American citizen. He pushed for all-out war against Germany and sought revenge against Germany for 1870.
Sir Douglas Haig (1861 – 1928) became British Commander-in-Chief in 1916 and alternatively disliked Lloyd George and Marshal Foch. Clemenceau also distrusted Foch as Allied command became an interwoven group of people who needed each other, but di not always get along.

296 – *King Alfonso of Spain upon his arrival with Queen Victoria at the famous Spanish watering place, San Sebastian, reviewing the Spanish troops who were lined up at the railway station in their majesty's honor. (Photo Central News)*

Alphonso XIII of Spain (1886-1941) was King of Spain from 1886 to 1936 when the Republic was proclaimed. Although Spain was neutral during World War I, the King was married to a granddaughter of Queen Victoria.

297 – *Robert Lansing, U.S. Secretary of State, and Lord Reading on their way to the White House to present the new British Ambassador's credentials to President Wilson.*

Robert Lansing (1864-1929) took over as Secretary of State following the resignation of William Jennings Bryan. He was originally in favor of neutrality, but soon found that difficult and started angling toward allying with Great Britain. He hired men for the newly formed Bureau of Secret Intelligence in 1916 to watch over agents of the Central Powers. He was influential in supporting independence for nationalities in the former Austro-Hungarian Empire.

298 – *Swordmaster with the sword of the Crown Prince of Japan. It must sever three stacks of bamboo and straw. (Theo. Moussault)*

The Crown Prince here is the future Emperor Hirohito (1901 – 1989) who ruled from 1926 -1989. Japan was one of the allied powers in the first world war. Japan took advantage of the war to seize German holdings in the far-east and China.

299 – *A most unusual and striking photograph of General Foch, generalissimo of all the Allied armies, and General Pershing, commander-in-chief of the American Expeditionary Forces, both wearing the smile of victory. When General Pershing offered the American army in France to General Foch, he accepted at once and manifested great appreciation. (Underwood and Underwood)*

Foch and Pershing did not always get along. The French Marshal wanted U.S. troops integrated into veteran British and French units, while Pershing insisted on the Americans serving together under a united command.

World War I through the Tabloids

300. *Secretary of War Baker at what he aptly termed, "the Frontier of Freedom", namely the front line American trenches in France. (Committee on Public Information)*

301. *Secretary Baker posing in uniform with a French general.*

Newton Baker was a politician and lawyer who was secretary of war from 1916 - 1921. He chose John J. Pershing to command the American Expeditionary Forces and insisted it should be an independent unit. He was often pictured in military uniform when among the troops.

302. *General Pershing giving final instructions to the officers of a Division about to leave for the Front Lines.*

Pershing fought to keep the AEF as an independent operational unit despite objections of French and British commanders.

The gentleman to the left of the picture in the fur coat is Douglas MacArthur.

303. *Capt Roald Amundsen, discoverer of the South Pole, photograph upon his arrival from the battle front in France. He had some very complementary things to say about the American troops he saw "over there" and sees nothing but victory for the Allied troops.*

Roald Amundsen was credited to reaching the South Pole in 1910 - 1912. Shortly after this picture was taken he left on a failed expedition to the North Pole that last to 1925. His plane disappeared on a rescue mission to the artic in 1928.

304. General Bouchier of the French Army who held a high command under General Petain at Verdun. He is very enthusiastic in his praise of American forces in France and says that with the aid of America's splendid army, the Allies will certainly win. (International Film Svc.)

305. *General Sir Henry Hughes Wilson, Chief of the British General Staff and military adviser to the Supreme War Council. Sir Henry is reputed to be a specialist on the war having realized its coming long before it actually materialized. (Photo International Film Svc)*

Sir Henry was instrumental in developing plans for the BEF in conjunction with the war staffs of France and Belgium. He was appointed to the Supreme War Council by Lloyd George. He was increasingly pessimistic about ending the war in 1918, and after the war remained a proponent of England's expanded role in world politics. He opposed Irish Independence and was assassinated by two IRA members in 1922.

306. *Lt. Colonel Milan Pribicevich, Head of the Serbian War Mission, who has returned to Europe to command more than 5,000 Southern Slav volunteers from America, for service on the Macedonian Front, the beginning of their participation in the war falling practically on Kossovo Day, the Serbian National Anniversary, observed today here and in many other large cities across the country.*

Kossovo Day is 28 June

Milan Pribicevich was a soldier in the Austrian army when he deserted to Serbia in 1904. He enlisted in the Serbian Army at the start of the Balkan Wars. He actively recruited American volunteers prior to the US's entry into the War. He died in 1937.

216   America at War

307. *Major General Sir George McMunn, K.C.B., D.S.O., Inspector General of Communications of the Mesopotamian Expeditionary Force (right) - one corner of the Turkish Prison camp at Basra.*

Sir George was later the High Commissioner of Palestine

308. *George Creel, Chairman of the Committee of Public Information, has been charged in Congress with making unpatriotic remarks and his removal has been demanded. (International Film Svc)*

The Committee of Public Information was set up after America entered the war as a propaganda agency of the government to promote the war effort, release news and administer voluntary press censorship, which Creel evidently administered with a light hand.

George Creel was a well-connected newspaperman prior to the war and remained at the head of the committee until its end in 1919. He died in 1953.

309. *This is Rep. Wm. P. Borland, of Kansas City who introduced the Daylight Saving bill in Congress, thereby being responsible for the whole nation getting out of bed an hour earlier than customary and having and extra hour in the afternoon.*

Borland was a Democrat who served in Congress from 1909 until his death in 1919 while in Germany.

World War I through the Tabloids

310/311. *General Ferdinand Foch.* "*My right and my left have been driven in. With what is left of the center I will attack.*" *is the message General Foch sent to headquarters just before the advance that turned the tide of the Battle of the Marne and saved Paris. This is the man who was chosen as the big boss of the allied armies.*

Foch joined the French army at the outbreak of the Franco-Prussian War and rose through the ranks. He was appointed Supreme Commander on 26 March 1918. He died in 1929

312 *General Petain, the French Commander-in-Chief, with hand at salute as the colors pass, reviewing his troops on the Western front a short time before the Germans launched their drive last March in the great Picardy battle. According to authentic information there are four million French soldiers now in France. German commanders openly admit that French troops are in every respect as well trained and efficient as their own, which has been abundantly proven in this greatest of wars. Now that French, British, American, Italian and Portuguese troops are all fighting as a unit and in an inspired way, Germany's chances of winning the war are very small, indeed. (Underwood and Underwood)*

Although Petain was viewed as a hero by the end of World War I, heading up the Vichy Government during World War II marred his reputation. His service during World War I probably saved him from execution.

313 – *Von Hindenberg and the Kaiser trying to decide how many more hundreds of thousands must be sacrificed for their personal ambitions. (Kadel & Herbert)*

There was very little sympathy for Germany or their leaders.

314. *General Herbert Plummer, of the British Army, and his officers, who two years ago captured Messines Ridge and who recently directed the defense of the same ridge, retiring before great odds. (Central News Photo Service, NY)*

315. *Premier Clemenceau of France (center) on the Flanders front. General Plummer of the British army (left) is explaining the military situation. (Underwood and Underwood)*

Hebert Plumer, (not Plummer) 1st Viscount Plumer (1857 - 1932), was the senior British Officer of the British Army in World War I. He commanded the V Corps at the second battle of Ypres in 1915 and took over the Second Army in May 1915, winning the Battle of Messines in 1917. He commanded the army during the German Spring Offensive and the Hundred Days Offensive. He was the Commander of the British Army of the Rhine, Governor of Malta and finally High Commissioner of Palestine in 1925.

Places

The war brought places of battle to the living rooms of Americans. For the previous three years Americans heard about places described in reports about the war.

316. *The Cathedral of Arras*

The Cathedral of Arras was originally built in the 11th century and constructed in its present form starting in 1755. The cathedral was listed as heavily damaged in April 1917 during the Nivelle Offensive, but there is a Pathe film from 1916 showing the cathedral already damaged. This was considered one of the great outrages of the war. It was rebuilt in its original form after the war.

317. *The Coliseum in Rome was used for a patriotic rally*

Prior to the 1930's the interior of the Coliseum was not excavated so that it was possible to stand on the arena floor. It was used for rallies full of people till that time.

318. *Fort Douamont at Verdun.* "*Unusual view of Fort Douamont, key position in the battle of Verdun*

Fort Douaumont was considered one of the strongest defensive fortifications along the French line. Specifically built to withstand 420mm Gama guns. It was quickly captured in February 1916 when one of the outer casement doors was left open. Some of the most brutal fighting of the war took place there until it was recapture in October 1916. Even though the battle had been over there for two years, it still evoked curiosity amongst readers.

319. The Moulin Rouge. "*The famous Moulin Rouge dance hall in Paris is now a storehouse for American army supplies. (International Film)*"

The Moulin Rouge was a nightclub that was founded in 1889 and famous for its wild nightlife. The original structure burned in 1915 and rebuilt in 1921. At the time US troops were in Paris it was not active, but the name was still well known.

320. St. Quentin. "*Street scene in St. Quentin during the first German occupation of the city, showing the civilian population being deported by the Huns. This historic place has been a German war base since the latter part of 1914 and is one of the points from which the German drive of 1918 started. Before the war it was a thriving city with a population of about 65,000. (International Film Service)*"

The population of St. Quentin was forced out of the city in March 1914 and the city was systematically looted. It was incorporated into the Hindenburg Line and sustained damage to over 80% of the city.

321. *A Section of the Somme battlefield near Peronne showing the character of the terrain over which hundreds of thousands of men have been battling for nearly four years and from which the British have been forced to retire in the great German drive of March. It is one of the most desolate places in northern France. (International Film)*

The first battle of the Somme was fought from July to November 1916 and the second battle was fought August to September 1918. It was some of the most devastated landscape on the western front where thousands were killed.

322. *In a cloister of Verdun*

The countryside of Verdun also saw devastation. Nothing in the path of battle was spared from destruction.

323. *All that is left of the foyer of the theatre at Rheims after months of bombardment by the Huns (Underwood and Underwood)*

Rheims was the site where the Kings of France were traditionally crowned in northern France. The damage to the cathedral was used by the allies as propaganda against the Germans for attacks on cultural landmarks.

324. *The ruins of Bapaume, an important town of Northern France which was overwhelmed by the great German advance of 1918, and which is here seen to be on fire. This place was captured from the British in night fighting after a sturdy and most bloody resistance in which the Germans, it is said lost 50,000 and the allies vast quantities of stores. (International Film Service) In August 1918 this was a focal point for the Battle of Amiens.*

Bapaume changed hands several times during the war. It was captured by the Germans in 1914, was the focus of the allies during the first Somme, captured by the British in 1917 and in March 1918 retaken by the Germans. During the second Battle of Bapaume, when this photo was taken (21 August – 3 September) it was part of the Hundred Days battles. Commonwealth troops broke through the German defenses, but Australians entering the town hall stumbled into a trap from a German mine timed to explode as they arrived. This photo could be from that event.

325. *British artillery crossing hastily made bridges over the Yser River to the scene of the recent battle in Flanders. (Underwood and Underwood)*

The Yser River was the scene of a battle in 1914 when the locals opened the sluice gates and slowed the German advance. By 1918, it was in some of the most fought over areas in northern France.

326. *Damaged French Chateau*

In a ruined landscape even old houses are not spared

327. *The ruin of war*

An unidentified hillside town destroyed. More than 26 villages and towns were destroyed during the war and never rebuilt.

328. *With the approach of dusk one evening a German patrol started across No Man's land to raid the French sector on the Champagne Front. They thought that by not waiting for complete darkness, they would catch the French napping, but the poilus were on guard and this remarkable photo shows the Frenchmen using their hand grenades with deadly effect against their Teutonic adversaries who were completely routed. (Underwood and Underwood)*

Most trench raids were carried out at night so that the opposing troops did not have a clear view. There was no such think as nighttime photography in 1918 so this could very well have been a staged photo or some other action that has been labeled as such.

BIBLIOGRAPHY

Abbott, P and Pinak, E. *Ukrainian Armies 1914-55*. (Osprey Publishing: Oxford). 2004

Bull, Dr. Stephen. *World War I Trench Warfare (1)*. (Osprey Publishing: Oxford). 2002

Burr, Lawrence. *British Battlecruisers 1914-18*. (Osprey Publishing: Oxford) 2006

Cornish, Nik. *The Russian Army 1914-18*. (Osprey Publishing: Oxford). 2001

Feltman, Brian K. "Tolerance as a crime? The British treatment of German prisoners of war on the Western Front, 1914-1918", *War in History* 17/4, 2010,

Gudmundsson, Bruce. *The British Army of the Western Front 1916*. (Osprey Publishing: Oxford).2007

Haythornthwaite, Philip J. *The World War One Source Book*. (Arms & Armor: London). 1994

Henry, Mark R. *The US Army of World War I*. (Osprey Publishing: Oxford). 2003

Henry, Mark R. *US Marine Corps in World War I 1917-18*. (Osprey Publishing: Oxford). 1999

Hoff, Thomas A. *US Doughboy 1916-19*. (Osprey Publishing: Oxford). 2005

Imperial War Museum. *German Military Terms, 1918*. (The Battery Press: Nashville) 1995

Jung, Peter. *The Austro-Hungarian Forces in World War I 1914-16 (1)*. (Osprey Publishing: Oxford) 2003

Lardas, Mark. *World War I Seaplane and Aircraft Carriers*. (Osprey Publishing: Oxford) 2016

Mead, Gary. *The Doughboys: America and the First World War*. (Overlook: New York) 2000

Miller, Dr. Christine and Dougherty, Dr. Paul, "The Perils and Progress of Trench Warfare: Battlefield Medicine During the First World War." *The Journal of America's Military Past.* Volume XLIV, Fall 2019, No. 3, pp. 23-31

Mollo, John and Turner, Pierre. *Army Uniforms of World War 1*. Arco Publishing Company: New York. 1978

Mortenson, Christopher R.; Springer, Paul J. *Daily life of U.S. Soldiers: from the American Revolution to the Iraq War*. (Santa Barbara, California: Greenwood). 2019

Nash, David. *German Infantry 1914-1918*. (Almark Publications: Edgeware) 1971

Nicolle, David. *The Italian Army of World War I*. (Osprey Publishing: Oxford). 2003

Pershing, John J. *My Experiences in the World War. Vol I, II* (Frederick A Stokes: New York). 1931

Phelan, Joseph A. *Heroes & Aeroplanes of the Great War 1914 – 1918*. (Grosset & Dunlap: New York). 1968

Quirini, Mjr. Eugenjusz I Librewski, Kpt. Stanisław. *Ilustrowana Kronika Legjonow Polskich 1914-18*. (Nakład Głównej Księgarni Wojskowej: Waszawa). 1936

Strachan, Hew. *The First World War*. (Simon & Schuster: New York). 2003

Strachan, Hew. *The First World War*. (Viking: New York). 2003

Strohn, Mathias ed., *World War I Companion*. (Osprey Publishing: Oxford). 2013

Summer, Ian. *German Air Forces 1914-18*. (Osprey Publishing: Oxford). 2005

Thomas, Nigel Phd. *The German Army in World War I 1914-15 (1)*. Osprey Publishing: Oxford). 2003

Thomas, Nigel Phd. *The German Army in World War I 1916-17 (2)*. Osprey Publishing: Oxford). 2003

Thomas, Nigel Phd. *The German Army in World War I 1917-18 (3)*. Osprey Publishing: Oxford). 2004

Votaw, John F. *The American Expeditionary Forces in World War I*. (Osprey Publishing: Oxford). 2005

Winter, J.M. *The Experience of World War I*. (Oxford University Press: New York). 1989

Zaloga, Steven. *German Panzers 1914-18*. (Osprey Publishing: Oxford). 2006

Accessed on-line:

https://www.kumc.edu/school-of-medicine/academics/departments/history-and-philosophy-of-medicine/archives/wwi/essays/medicine/gas-in-the-great-war.html#:~:text=The%20minimal%20immediate%20effects%20are,%2C%20diphosgene%20(trichloromethane%20chloroformate).

https://www.bbc.com/news/magazine-31042472

America at War
Sources

Here is a list of the sources the images in this book came from where they could be identified

Bain News Service – was started by George Grantham Bain in 1898. He was known as "the father of foreign photographic news". The photographs Bain produced and gathered for distribution through his news service were worldwide in their coverage, but there was a special emphasis on life in New York City. The bulk of the collection dates from the 1900s to the mid-1920s, but scattered images can be found as early as the 1860s and as late as the 1930s.

British Pictorial Service – photography services provided by the British Government

Central News Service - The Central News Agency was a news distribution service founded as Central Press in 1863 by William Saunders and his brother-in-law, Edward Spender. In 1870–71, it adopted the name Central News Agency. By undercutting its competitors, the Press Association and Reuters, and by distributing sensational and imaginative stories, it developed a reputation amongst newsmen for "underhand practices and stories of dubious veracity". During the war it was run by Henry McAuliffe (later Sir), with John Gennings as Manager.

Commission of the Gas Defense Service – government commission that explored the effects of gas in warfare

Committee of Public Information - (1917–1919), also known as the CPI or the Creel Committee, was an independent agency of the government of the United States under the Wilson administration created to influence public opinion to support the US in World War I, in particular, the US home front. In just over 26 months, from April 14, 1917, to June 30, 1919, it used every medium available to create enthusiasm for the war effort and to enlist public support against the foreign and perceived domestic attempts to stop America's participation in the war. It is a notable example of propaganda in the United States. Domestic activities stopped after the Armistice was signed on November 11, 1918. Foreign operations ended June 30, 1919. Wilson abolished the CPI by executive order 3154 on August 21, 1919. On August 21, 1919, the disbanded organization's records were turned over to the Council of National Defense.

French Official Photographs – photography services provided by the French Government

International Film Service - In 1914, William Randolph Hearst expanded his International News Service wire syndicate into the International Picture Service, a syndicate formed to create newsreels, when newsreels were an entirely new idea. The success of the Hearst Newsreel led the media magnate to create International Film Service (IFS) in 1915. The studio did give birth to one enduring series, however: Krazy Kat. World War I proved the death-knell for IFS. Hearst had been pursuing an aggressive pro-German position for decades under the assumption that German immigrants were the core of his newspaper consistency. As a result, International News Service lost its credibility. The spiraling debt this created forced Hearst to cut out his least-profitable business, and that was IFS. The entire staff was laid off on July 6, 1918, a date referred to in animation history as "Black Monday".

International News Service - Established two years after Hearst-competitor E.W. Scripps combined three smaller syndicates under his control into United Press Associations, INS battled the other major newswires. It added a picture service, International News Photos, or INP. The Hearst newsreel series Hearst Metrotone News (1914–1967) was released as International Newsreel from January 1919 to July 1929. Universal Service, another Hearst-owned news agency, merged with International News Service in 1937. INS was merged with UP on May 24, 1958, to become UPI. During the early years of World War I, Hearst's INS was barred from using Allied telegraph lines, because of how it reported British losses.

Italian War Photos – photography services provided by the Italian Government

Kadel & Herbert - Kadel & Herbert News Feature Photo Service was a photographic news service in New York City, a partnership of George J. Kadel and Edward J. Herbert

Moussault, Theo (1888 - 1974) a Dutch photographer

Newark Evening News - was an American newspaper published in Newark, New Jersey. As New Jersey's largest city, Newark played a major role in New Jersey's journalistic history. At its apex, The News was widely regarded as the newspaper of record in New Jersey

Press Illustrating Service

Ruschin, Henry (1890 – 1970) American photographer

Times Photo Service – The *New York Times* photography

Underwood & Underwood - The company was founded in 1881 in Ottawa, Kansas, by two brothers, Elmer Underwood and Bert Elias Underwood. They moved to Baltimore and then to New York City in 1891. At one time, Underwood & Underwood was the largest publisher of stereoviews in the world, producing 10 million views a year. By 1910, Underwood & Underwood had entered the field of news photography. The company ceased business in the 1940s.

Western Newspaper Union – A Chicago based newspaper chain

The World

Wyndham Press Service

Other images used:

Army Camps in the US During World War I, on page 6 is from Wikipedia
Europe in 1914, on page 23 is from Wikipedia
Post Card on page 86 is from the editor's collection

Look for more books from Winged Hussar Publishing, LLC – E-books, paperbacks and Limited-Edition hardcovers. The best in history, science fiction and fantasy at:
https://www. wingedhussarpublishing.com
or follow us on Facebook at:
Winged Hussar Publishing LLC
Or on twitter at:
WingHusPubLLC
For information and upcoming publications

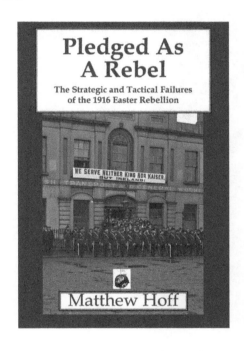

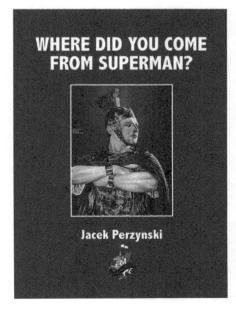